"You Suck!"

Have you ever said that to yourself?

How To Turn Your Lying Fraidy-Cat Inner Critic

Into a Confident, Courageous Fan

Valery Satterwhite

ISBN: 0982187815

ISBN-13: 9780982187814

DEDICATION

This book is dedicated to you. You are excellence in motion.
Embrace your magnificence. Step into it so you become the very
thing you hold in your dreams.

And to my husband, Al Satterwhite, my inspiration and champion,
who saw and cheered my authentic greatness before
we shared our first bottle of wine.

CONTENTS

INTRODUCTION

You Suck!

How many times have you said that to yourself? How many times has your self-doubt motivated you to **F**ind **E**xcuses **A**nd **R**easons (FEAR) why you can't be, do or have what your heart desires?

There's only one thing standing in the way of the life you dream of. There's only one thing that prevents you from being who you long to be. There's only one thing that stops you from having the confident courage to achieve authentic greatness with unrelenting drive and passion.

That Thing Is...YOU!!

Well, one part of you. And that's the egoistic Inner Critic who holds you back, and keeps you in an unfulfilling comfort zone. The zone, the place you're in right now, is familiar to you. Even if you don't like your current circumstances, they're what you know and are therefore safe.

To keep you right where you are your Inner Critic serves up lie after lie after lie to stop you in your tracks, make you doubt your potential and fear anything that's outside the comfy blanket of your conditioning.

You Suck! She lied.

And you remain stuck, unfulfilled, depleted of life-affirming energy and inspiration.

A life unfulfilled is a life of quiet desperation. You feel there's something missing. Yet that something seems vague and elusive. There's nothing missing inside of you. There's nothing you need that isn't already there, nothing you could want that hasn't always been there. Life has a funny way of showing up, and people have a silly way of pretending that they can duck and cover when it does in unexpected ways.

But what if, instead of always waiting for life to show up, you sprinted forward into the parts of life that you were born to experience and achieve? Sure, you'll stumble a time or two; you may even fall flat on your butt during the most embarrassing of circumstances. Those events are gifts, just like raindrops or snowy February mornings. Why would you want to skip those miracles?

Imagine for a moment what life would be like if you were the master of your opportunities instead of the victim of your circumstances?

Who do you think you are, a Superstar? Well, how right you are! (Thank you, John Lennon)

There is a superstar, an Einstein, a Spielberg, a Richard Branson, an Oprah Winfrey, a Steve Jobs or a Craig Ferguson living inside of you just waiting to be unleashed. There's also a very frightened, confused and grumpy part of you who would argue that I'm insane. But then there's the part of you who already knows that I speak the truth. Which one of them wears the pants in your life? Which one directs your personal power and truth?

Bob Dylan said it best: "When you feel in your gut who you are and dynamically pursue it—don't back down and don't give up—you're going to mystify a lot of folks."

YOU are here to mystify a lot of folks.

In order to do that, you've got to take away the power that woefully misguided Inner Critic has over you so you can **Moxie Up!**

> *Moxie is the confident courage to achieve authentic greatness with unrelenting drive and passion.*

Without further ado, it's my privilege and honor to help guide you to the power you already have within you so you can bring out the magnificent being you are. Your ultimate life purpose and birthright is: THE FREEDOM AND EXPRESSION OF YOUR FULL AUTHENTIC POTENTIAL. When you learn to **Moxie Up!** you become the master of every opportunity instead of the depleted victim of your circumstances. You bring forth out into the open the star, the shining light, that you're here to be.

If I could give you just one gift, I would give you the ability to see yourself as I see you, so you could see how truly special you are. When you can show up in your life with Moxie—the fortitude, guts, chutzpah, confidence and commitment to the magnificence that is you and your deepest desires—you will:

Claim your truth. Own your power. Command your stage.

To the extent that you don't feel satisfied or don't like who you are, you've given your Moxie over to your Inner Critic. With that power, your Inner Critic beats the drum of lies, lies and more lies about you and your opportunities.

Why? Because she's scared and wants you to keep her company in her fear and self-doubt. When you examine how she's been holding you back you'll learn how to reclaim your truth, power, passionate pursuit and achievement of your life-affirming purpose.

You will never again say to yourself…

CHAPTER ONE

YOU SUCK!

"Who Do You Think You're Kidding...
You're Nothing But A Failure...
You're Not Smart Enough...
You're Not Good Looking Enough...
Talented Enough...
Old Enough...
Young Enough...
Rich Enough...
Connected Enough...
Trained Enough...
Brave Enough...
You Are Not Enough!"

You are Not enough to be, do or have what you want to achieve and experience in life.

So Forget It!

Crawl back under the protective blanket of your unauthentic life, your conditioning, and go back to your old familiar ways because YOU SUCK, and that's all you'll ever be good at—sucking.

Forget about what you long to do. You can't have it.

Accept your mediocrity. Blame other people and other things for your inability to move forward in your own life. And have a nice friggin' day.

If any of the above sounds familiar, if this is the story you tell yourself about yourself day after day, or at least in times of potentially life changing challenges, then your Inner Critic rules you. She's the voice of your self-doubt and fear. And she LIES!

LIES!! All Lies!

Why?

Because she's a scared shitless little thing that sits comfy in the sandbox of your mind and wants you to stay right there with her. She's not going anywhere, so why should you?

Yet your heart calls for something else…

Another life.

The life you know, deep down inside, you were born to have…

"Please, help me," you cry inside, "it's *Got* to get better than this!"

And it can.

You were born with unconditional love of everyone else and of yourself. You knew, without question, that you were connected to everyone else through love. When you started to feel separated from everyone else, you created your Inner Critic who, with her Rule Book, was charged with keeping you safe in a disconnected, unattached world. Judgment entered your life and made itself more than comfortable. It became a staple diet. You viewed yourself and your life experiences as better than or lesser than those you knew. You became attached to that which you thought would keep you safe. You began to fight for your existence, for that which you already had at birth—Unconditional Love.

You forgot that you're an alchemist, a **WIZARD**! You have the **W**isdom, **I**ntuition, **Z**eal, **A**uthenticity, **R**esponsibility and **D**ecisiveness within you to create any experience you choose. This is your True Self. As the confident courageous WIZARD of creativity that she is, her essence resides in your heart. The outer expression of the all-knowing inner bundle of pure authentic passion and energy is, what I playfully call, **MOXIE!**

And you've been fighting for it ever since.

Your heart is calling, begging you to **Moxie Up!**—to boldly and authentically live out loud. This is the longing you have deep within your soul. You know it's there. You can feel it. It's the part of you that wishes to be more. It wants more because you are much bigger than you've allowed yourself to reveal. The inner calling is the real you. As the messenger of your authentic truth and wisdom, she's always been there as your personal guidance system, directing you through intuition, good feelings and authenticity.

Your Inner Critic has been giving you marching orders so loudly you haven't heard, let alone paid any attention, to the voice of your own inner truth. The intuitive voice of your Inner Being, your True Self, who is there to show you how to confidently express who you really are to bring forth what you really want into reality.

The guidance provided by your True Self is your birthright. Learn how to calm the Inner Critic and empower who you *really* are, to confidently express your full potential… your unique purpose in life.

> *Thinking, speaking and boldly acting in alignment with who you really are and what you really want is MOXIE.*

Empower your authenticity and follow your natural, light, positive energy and laugh at, to, about and with yourself. The Inner Critic is a stubborn, misguided entity when empowered, and she doesn't go softly into any good night… so what can you do with her?

She's like the cranky old lady who wanders into the same coffee shop every day just to annoy and pester that poor waitress who can never seem to get her order right. Just when this waitress thinks she knows exactly what that old bag will have and how she'll take it, the old lady gripes and complains and makes her start all over again. It's a daily habitual routine that the two of them would be lost without.

All she wants to do, the overworked waitress tells herself, is to get a better job (the last of which really sucked the life out of her). Or maybe she wants to break free of the employee restraints and go after her entrepreneurial dream. She's gotten some pretty good feedback from some pretty important people, and she just wants to be sure before she ditches the café for the big time only to find herself bar tending within the week for extra cash, back to the same old same old life, only the location has changed.

She'll be ready soon, she tells herself, and once she's pouring Long Islands instead of bitter lattés, all the right doors will fly open, she'll make more money or get a new job offer where she'll meet better people and finally be catapulted into the world where she belongs. But the gnarly, grouchy, frightened Inner Critic just knocks the wind right out of her sails. She takes her focus off of the true task at hand and grumbles her way about the place, complaining, wasting her time, wasting her resources and driving herself absolutely nuts. "Who are you kidding?" she screams within her head. "Who do you think you are, a superstar?"

Well, how right you are. The voice of your True Self will remind you that, Yes you are, indeed, a superstar.

> *"Deep down inside, you know there's something more powerful within you begging you to bring it out into the world. Dare to let it come out and play fully expressed."*

If you're unfulfilled you have three choices. First, you could resign yourself to the life long dance of never getting it right, never feeling truly good about even the simplest of your creations, even with three teaspoons of sugar and a dash of cream. (The Inner Critic wants you to fold and retreat; it's much safer, less embarrassing.) Second, you could become extremely rude, bitter and angry, cussing and cursing her out, expending priceless energy beating yourself up over and over again to no avail.

You think your Inner Critic is a permanent fixture. She's been with me for years. She'll never go away! She'll never change, you sadly remind yourself. Yes, the Inner Critic is a part of you, misguidedly conditioned by her early childhood environment to keep you safe in your now shrunken little world, held back by negative energy and emotionally expensive experiences. Like a vital organ, you can't get rid of her. Like a vital organ, you don't want to get rid of her. Being aware of her voice and her real intentions will help you decide whether the thought you're having or the decision you're about to make will take you closer (inspiration) or further (fear) from your goals.

Here's your third choice: you could disarm her with love and kindness. Acknowledge and humor her. Finally take back the power she has over you, teach her a few new, more supportive tricks and transform her harsh, nitpicky ways into something that serves as an intuitive reminder that if you follow this negative pull you'll head down a backward path. The more you mindfully take away the power your Inner Critic has over you the more she'll become a confident courageous fan.

Serve her with a smile, understanding that she is who she is, a frightened little child still trying to cope in an environment that's no longer relevant. Stand centered your authenticity—the truth of who you are and what would rock your world.

Make the well-meaning yet lost inner part of you far less powerful by staying acutely aware of the signals she serves up in the form of limiting, smothering beliefs and exhausting, exasperating life drama. By paying attention to how you feel in any given moment, you as the creator of all that is delicious will know if you've turned back to your old, tired routine of "never good enough," or if you're headed—inspired and full of Moxie—in the direction of passionately pursuing the life of your dreams.

Simply put, if you're miserable and exhausted, you're back on the habitual treadmill toward nowhere; the path of blown careers and missed opportunities. However, if you're feeling good, you're expressing your Moxie—your birthright power to create your own authentic experience—rather than embodying the haggard results of the power that others, and your own Inner Critic, have had over you.

Deliver yourself into a new, energizing daily routine of personal awareness and power, through which you make yourself stronger, happier and more able to offer positive light to the dreariest of situations and people. Which one will you choose? Will you boldly take that step, own your truth, reclaim your power and venture into a new world of possibilities, no matter how scary it may be at times? Or will you remain a victim to the bully within who blames everything on you and outer circumstances?

Bullies only bully for the reaction they get, of the "powerful" feeling they achieve when they make someone cry or when they cause upset. This feeling is a transference and release of their own pain, confusion and fear. They have an intuition about who the weak ones are, and about how to hit them where it hurts. That's the only way they know how to stay in control.

Bullies are too afraid to give up control and they confuse power with force. There are those who will pay the bully's way through school with surrendered lunch money and forged essays, and there are those who the bully will rarely get a rise out of. Are you the picked on, the timid, the one boiling over inside with silent pain, desperation and fear? Or are you the one who's untouchable, inspirational, meandering about with a confidence and glow that pulls people and good feelings toward you?

The Inner Critic is a bully just the same, and those who allow themselves to be controlled by her will remain in the victim stance until they learn that the Moxie—the self-confidence and self-love—can conquer just about any obstacle or tragedy and master any opportunity. You don't have to earn that freedom, or find it, or wish for it or wait until you deserve it. It's been with you all along. It's your birthright.

This is the difference between Powerless Living and Living with Power. Your Inner Critic mirrors and reiterates every danger and negative impulse that it believes the world has to offer, and in that way, she'll never shut up and let you be, serving up a steaming heap of Powerless Living at every turn. If you've given into her and her constant nagging, swallowed what she served, you've given power over to fear and negativity. Soon, this is all you'll be able to see. Everyone will be out to get you, everyone will be to blame, you'll be to blame, everything will be a scam and too difficult to attain and you'll be a steaming pile of cow dung because the world says so.

> *"The expiration date on blaming your parents, other people and other things for your misfortune is long past."*

Crappy job, crappy life, trapped, uninspired, blocked, imprisoned, going nowhere fast, back hurts, can't quit smoking because of the stress that the crappy world puts on you. Too much traffic, not enough creative vision, no time, debt that would give an elephant a stroke, not enough money for the high-end designer tchotchkes you drool over, grumpy spouse, kid's in trouble at school, can't write a tune let alone dance to your own, that jackass got the cover page you deserved… UUGGHHHH!!! *Isn't it Exhausting?* You're being bullied, from the inside out and it's left you utterly spent and hopeless. Or so you think…

This is where I want to speak frankly with you, just for a minute… because I was the Queen of quiet desperation. I was lonely for something I didn't even know existed. I beat the bloody hell out of myself and those around me for not knowing what I wanted or how to get it. I had built a life around myself, a seemingly enviable life by materialistic standards, that I just didn't want. The realization that, since I had placed my own identity, dreams, hopes, truth and creative passions on the back burner, I had nothing at all in common with my first husband. Our life together became overwhelming and I begun an ill-fated journey in hopes of sabotaging my marriage.

Of course, I didn't see it that way while I was doing it, but I was just too weak and ashamed to say, "Hey, maybe we could cut the strings that bind us on good terms. We don't need to pretend anymore. I'd love to still keep you as the friend and confidant you've always been." No… not me… not the confused, frightened, rebellious woman who didn't know how to change her life, how to go from being a quiet bored-to-tears Washington DC lobbyist's wife and technology marketer to a wonderfully stylish, whimsically creative, inspiring, larger than life person I knew was inside without causing an ugly exit.

I was unable to stand strong in the truth of who I was, and I didn't know how to dig the real me out from beneath the "should be" life that smothered me. So I blew up my seemingly farcical existence in order to break free. That way, I had no choice other than to start rebuilding and reshaping from the ground up. I literally disintegrated the safety net. There was a gift for me in that fall from grace. I learned that I wouldn't die. I discovered I could flourish, without the safety net.

> *"You can build a solid foundation upon rock-bottom."*

If this is where you think you are, I completely understand, and I'm here to tell you that your fears are founded in your "perceived" reality, and it's not an inescapable one. If the information you've absorbed thus far has started to move and inspire you and reintroduce you to the Inner Being, your Inner Critic is most definitely jumping in at every turn. She's chatting your ear off about all the trouble and inconvenience that's in store for you should you decide to deviate from the entrapment plan she has buffaloed you into.

After I blew up my Washington DC life, I moved to New York City with my heart glowing afire. On the plane and upon my arrival at La Guardia airport, my soul was screaming, "I've arrived!" I remember walking aimlessly through those bustling streets looking for a place to live with her yelling in my ear, "What in the hell have you done? We're gonna Die! Brilliant!" My Inner Critic's frightful reality sunk in.

The relationships and responsibilities you've built up around you are very real, and though they may seem to be holding you back from your dreams, they aren't. You're the only one who can do that, and you've become very good at it. You don't have to storm out of your workplace, divorce your spouse, desert your children, tell your parents off and fly off to an exotic place where nobody knows your name in order to see your dreams and authentic life unfold. All you have to do is trust and allow yourself to be guided by your True Self, and a peaceful resolution to everything around you will start to prevail.

> *"By whatever name you call it, inner power is the intuitive creative force behind joyful 'in the zone' moments of fulfillment."*

There's no need for you to blow up your life. All you need to think about is showing up differently to it each day. Show up as a leader, an innovator, brilliant artist, an authentic wonder who's centered in the truth of who you are. Let that poor, sad, victim of circumstance fall to the wayside and learn how it's done. You created the side of yourself that's a victim of circumstance through the prompting and deafening negativity of your Inner Critic. You're the only one who can direct which foot you put forward in every situation. Without exception, if you show up differently, the circumstances surrounding and stemming from your life will be different.

It's far more productive, and less painful, to allow the changes that you'll realize flow through you and out into the world. This positive glow and drive will emanate from you to help those around you to recognize something in themselves that they too were ignoring. Just as the Inner Critic is drawn to and draws in negative, have-to situations, the True Expressive Self is drawn to and draws in positive, light-hearted and adventurous optimism. This is the yin and yang inside of you, and it's always been your choice which way you viewed yourself and the road you've taken. You have a brilliant and unique power within you—

your Moxie, your true birthright. Yet so many have forgotten how to be guided by it and have lost their way along with their innate Moxie power.

The past has given you perceptions and one-sided memories that cause you to give your power over to the doubtful and pessimistic Inner Critic, but that's not who you truly are. You're much less complex, thus far more miraculous, than that. Now, the new way of showing up in your life takes a bit of redirected natural energy, at first. Remember, living life against your nature has taken far more energy and strength for a far longer stretch of your life. Soon you'll find yourself working effortlessly toward something greater rather than struggling hard just to keep your head above water.

Living life according to your nature energizes and inspires you, and those around you will begin to relate differently to you as a result. Living against your nature has been exhausting and deflating, and those around you have recognized and reiterated that negativity as a means of communicating with, relating to and gaining power over you. *Aren't you sick and tired of being sick and tired?*

So, what would happen if your spouse decided that he/she wanted to start that same old fight about money (get a Real J.O.B.) or mud on the carpet, and you decided that he/she deserved acknowledgement for their concerns rather than the usually balling out in return? Offering acknowledgement, compassion and understanding doesn't mean you've given in to the Inner Critic wiles and ways of another.

It merely means you recognize the voice of an Inner Critic, whether it be your own or someone else's. You understand that, though it's magnified and misguided, it means well. By responding with calm understanding, you're able to bring your own truth forward in a way that's conceivable and understandable, too. Is there a way of addressing and calming the concerns of the other person without sacrificing or putting off your own truth and chosen path?

Yes, there's absolutely, always a way. Acknowledge the other person's concerns, whether they're real to you or not, even if they seem miniscule and steeped in negative energy. Respond with your own truth, finding a place where both truths can be honored. If this isn't possible, you have to draw the line and not cross your personal boundaries. There are things that are in alignment with who you are, and there are things that are not. It's not about compromising on a vacation to Hawaii instead of Paris. It's about compromising on who you are at the deepest core.

The difference is distinct and profound and can be measured by the feelings you get when you a make a concession. Clear indicators of an unnatural, forced compromise from your authentic self and natural flow will be exhausting and you'll be slipping back into that tired old safety routine which has gotten you nowhere. Indicators of clear and necessary compromise will find all parties satisfied and content, taking very little energy from you or your cause.

You can't change people, or the way they think or feel about you or themselves, by force. You think you can mold, shape, discipline, remind or coax until they bend to your will… but you Simply Cannot. Just as you're learning now about your True Self, and about those things that no amount of life or rules or time has changed about you, you're learning that everyone is who they are. You may be able to box them into your way of thinking for some amount of time, but you'll be nurturing resentment and feelings of anger.

The only way to allow peace and true authenticity to reign seamlessly through your life is to lead the way by example. If you change the way you interact with others and yourself, others will change the way they feel about you and themselves. And if the bitterness persists, or the gulf can't be bridged via the glow and positive energy you exude, then that's just the way it is. Keep yourself open to reconciliation, but move forward happily upon your quest. They'll catch up. Or not. What you can change is the experience you have with other people as a result of their comments and actions and what you believe they mean about you.

It's a funny thing, too, as you change the way you show up in your life, others tend to change the way they show up when they're around you. Like an audience clapping for an encore, soon everyone around you will be happily clapping to your refreshing, catchy beat. Rock On!

Of course… you could always just… procrastinate? Sure, why not? Let's talk about that for a little while, shall we?

CHAPTER TWO

YOU CAN'T!

"The human spirit is like a shark.
It has to constantly move forward or it dies."

The preponderance of ponderousness. Just thinking about it gives me a headache. You're inwardly tormented between longing to do something and talking yourself out of it. So you end up doing nothing but filling time with activities that just keep you stuck in not getting anywhere land.

There are times when doing nothing is just what we need to be doing, as in the "swinging with the breeze in a hammock" kind of nothing. But then there are the nothings that weigh so heavily and call so desperately... Change! Action! Lightning! Anything! Let me feel Something, Please!

The Inner Critic calls it boredom, normal, and tells you to shake it off, suck it up and get ready for the next set of nothings, because that's all life is made of. "I know!" she proclaims, "you should numb your own voice, desires and hunger by losing yourself in a story or some sort of mindless drivel on the boob tube. That'll get your head right."

Oh, great. Fan-Friggin-Tastic. Let's do that some more. Let's rant and rave inside, push our calm, gentle, natural gut feelings away and focus on Somebody Else. Don't get me wrong, I love a good success story, and I've had my fair share of desires to be another Oprah Winfrey, Angelina Jolie or a female version of Richard Branson or Steve Jobs. There's a lot of inspiration to be had through those who live such extraordinary lives. Your challenge, though, is to find your own inspiration and to listen for your own authentic identity and voice through what will rock your world and make your heart sing.

It's okay to idolize those heroes who kept you entertained and feeling good about yourself. But when you try to replace your own callings, your own Dreams, with the creations, lives, romances and dramas of others just to escape what you don't know how to fix, you're Doing Nothing. A fat lot of nothing… the bad kind. You're doing nothing with your natural gifts, your purpose in life.

And there's also the kind of nothing that doesn't at all feel like nothing. When you're running circles around yourself, doing "meaningful, important work" that drains and stupefies you day in and day out, the Inner Critic thinks it's really something. To her, the harder you work at something, the more real results will show up. Make no mistake, though, it's still nothing. It isn't yours, and you don't like it, or want it or particularly care who benefits from it.

You may get really good at nothing; I know I was good—really good. I was a top notch, well paid, professional, smart-as-a-whip nothing doer. But mostly I wondered, when does the nothing end? If there's no finishing point, no place that I'm aiming to get to, how do I know when my time of doing nothing is over? Do I just drop dead of exhaustion? Is that to be my fateful end?

> *"Be mindful of other people's thoughts in your head masquerading as yours."*

If someone had told me then that I was bludgeoning myself over the head with my own tools, I would never have listened. I would never have believed. I was good, and all set, and that was just a long, drawn out phase, or so I believed. And the world was just running its course around, under, over and on top of me. What could one person do against all that responsibility and weight? Why should I feel guilty for that which wasn't in my control? How could one little person shift the world over and force it to sit at bay?

> *"Anything in your way that seems like an obstacle or a detour really is an opportunity in disguise to show your resourcefulness."*

Everything would be okay soon, I said to myself, and all of my heavy dreaming, all my best gifts and brightest instincts would simply pop back out of me when they were ripe and ready. If I stopped wringing my hands, pounding my head and pulling my hair out, I would wake up one day to find that finished, polished and pristine Me. It would be magical, like a white Pegasus unicorn swooping in to carry me out of my lonely hell and take me to a place where I fit in, where I belonged. Of course, those dreamy, amazing Christian Louboutin shoes might be just as grand... maybe I could find the real Me shopping for those.

The problem with this? Well, for one... what am I, a pear? A banana? People don't sit on windowsills in paper bags until they're sweet and soft enough to eat... once we fall off the tree we're on our own. We either take root and bloom or we rot and turn into compost. And as for the other, well that's just ridiculous. The only way to get things done is to get going and do them. Period. There's no other way. Pegasus unicorn? Maybe, but I have to weigh in on the side of "Doubt It".

What truly surprised me, though, is how utterly exhausted I was. My "meaningful, important" job wasn't physically demanding, and my marriage, though strained, didn't usually demand too much of my time either. I came and went as I pleased, off on business trips to New York and Japan, back for a day or two and, Poof! Gone again. Perfect. I loved the travel. But inside, I was completely lost. I couldn't find, let alone express, my Moxie. I was so far away from thinking, speaking and acting in alignment with who I longed to become. Heck, it no longer occurred to me that I once knew who I wanted to be!

I felt desperate. I couldn't see Me, the dancer, the Eloise, the Pippi Longstocking, the Auntie Mame, anymore. Those were literary characters I adored and longed to be just like when I was a child. Without them talking to me, bubbling in me, calling me to come out and play, I felt just plain robotic. All these places, and these people and the impressive clientele I had garnered... I didn't care. Without Me there to enjoy the accomplishments, there was no feeling of success or completion.

What did I do when I wasn't working or traveling? Good question. Well... let's see...

Aahhh... that brilliant flash of genius. Contemplation. Meticulous planning. Organization. Excitement. Readying. Steadying. Perfected Internally. Meditation. More Coffee. Brief phone call... turned 63 minutes... and Counting... Bu-Bye now.... Crap, where'd I'd put that confounded train of thought?... Oh yeah, there you are! On to reckoning. Slight confusion... how the heck was that supposed to fly? Pondering. Pacing. Questioning. Advanced confusion. Deflation. Heated argument with self (aloud)... Exhaustion. Trash It.

All I got when I tried to fix the world around me was an even greater feeling of suffocation and confusion... meek and kind on the outside, screaming and ranting at the core. The proof was in the pudding, and I didn't even have a recipe for pudding. I was a mad person, churning over the stove with a fork, a plate and a craving, waiting for my yummy, tasty dreams to plop out of the range hood.

> *"Many of the things you want or think you need are really dead weights that serve as prisons you create for yourself."*

I was so disappointing to myself. I was that person who looks in the mirror, shakes her head and says, "What the hell happened to you? You used to be so cool, and you knew who you were... Where's your style? Where's your charisma? Where's that light?" Nobody had to say it, though some inadvertently did. Those dreaded questions from old friends and family; "Do you still dance?" or "Really? Information technology? Huh..." or "What happened to your sense of style? You used to be so fresh and quirky!"

Oh, nice. I had begun to look the way I felt. I exuded quiet defeat and a hard earned tolerance for life. The thing about it was I was setting myself up every day to run the same circle, to pace the same trail, to accomplish the same thing. Nothing.

What was I trying to do? I'm not really sure, to tell you the truth. Dreaming, I guess. The life of a dreamer acting with decisive intention is brilliant when effortlessly lived out loud. There's no skipping the work, the pain, the failure, the roller coaster that's a life spent struggling to find your unique expression, your gift, after it has been smothered and mangled by the strict nurturer.

There's also no escaping the utter confusion, desperation and trapped feeling of a stuck life ruled by the confused reluctant Inner Critic. Wake up to the fact that your Inner Being is just as big, even more powerful and has been right there with you all the while. Your True Self by definition has always known who you truly are, and has been trying to remind you for years and years. "Can you hear me Now?" she beacons calmly. "I'm just… right.. here, shift a little to the left. Yup. See, was that so hard?" Sometimes all it takes is a subtle shift in perspective.

It was during those times of frustration and chaos that my Inner Being, my True Self, was trying to break free, but of course I had no idea. All I felt was wrong, negative and ungrateful for my surroundings. I realize now that those feelings were the work of my Inner Critic, fighting tooth and nail to keep my dreams from surfacing and creating the uncertain reality that she so badly feared. Step away from the security of a paying job? Do something that you may not be recognized for? Trade the stuffy, high-class executive for a happy nobody? What about houses, cars, trips? What about Stability? You can't Do This! I won't let you Do This!

> *"When you step on the brakes, your life is in your foot's hands."*
> *-George Carlin*

I began to take a long look back, at all of the people and situations I'd met along the way and try to decide where I'd left myself behind. I'd been fascinated and enthralled by the energy, vitality and magic of New York City for decades. Auntie Mame lived in the city and fabulous, creative people, fashion and intimate, thrilling parties always surrounded her… I wanted that. And I did go to New York City, back and forth for business. I eventually moved there on my own to try my hand. Somehow, Auntie Mame had made it look so romantic, fun and easy, with her cocktails and humor, but once I got there to stay, I freaked out.

I mean, I literally freaked the heck out. My mortgage payment on a very nice townhouse in Washington, DC had been less than what they wanted me to pay to lease a 14x14 foot cell. No light, no room, no view… just a place where I had shelter from the rain and the Chinese delivery guy could find me. After wandering about aimlessly along those bustling streets asking myself, "Self? What In The Hell were you Thinking? What Do We Do Now?" I managed to calm down, pool my resources and started to think a bit more clearly. Wait… back up. Calm down? Calm, resources, clear thinking? Where in the world could that mentality possibly have come from? I was stranded, single and miserable in the one place I knew I would be happy if I could just get there!

Maybe, just maybe, that calm prevailed because no matter what the material or physical outcome of the choice I had made, I had finally pointed my arrow in the direction of my dreams. Just because we follow what we think will make us happy doesn't guarantee that we'll always come out smelling like roses. Stink bombs and failures are a certainty in all that we do.

But, if we're listening to what our authentic self has been trying to say, and we go with our guts, then crisis can and will be handled calmly, rationally and with a certain inner amusement. When you're sick and tired of being sick and tired, yet there's little room left for bitterness and regret… this is how you know when you're finished doing nothing. The wonderful, life affirming, soothing guidance of the True Self has finally been called into play.

> *"You have the power to step away from the titanic struggle with demons of insecurity any time you choose."*

CHAPTER THREE

YOU MUST FIT IN!

"The most beautiful thing that we can experience is the mysterious. It is the source of all art and science." -Albert Einstein

Welcome to your brain, the most grand and beautiful mystery of life. It's born of natural traits that are meant to shape and direct you toward the wonderfully unique individual you are to become (i.e., you started dancing, bopping and keeping rhythm before you could even walk = hint! hint!). Maybe you could outdraw your eight-year-old brother before you were three, or perhaps you learned to read and write on your own before you started school. Animals, even the most timid or aggressive, were innately drawn to you. Maybe you were happy, perky, athletic, prone to creating and solving equations. There have been clues that you were something special, authentic, beautiful, complete and wonderful since the very beginning.

Your magnificent brain also develops response, defense and safety triggers that are nurtured as you grow, and these are designed to help you adjust to your childhood, society and the environment you share with those around you. (You were told, "Children would kill for that food in Africa. You will clean that plate! This has left you feeling guilty and selfish about food and most of your motives every single day since, even though you were incapable of helping those poor children at the age of seven. Mayday! After all, you can't only share, can you? If you don't balance sharing with receiving, the pot will soon enough go empty, and nobody will be the better for your sacrifices in the end.) What's more, these nurtured behaviors are often in direct conflict with your natural abilities and gifts. In that sense, you have a sort of split personality issue that constantly conflicts with itself. Ah, isn't it wonderful?

And herein lies the mystery. You now have your true, authentic self, ripe for the picking, readily available at all times, and she's your true Inner Being. There's no ego here, no harshness, no excuses, no selfishness... your True Self and all her wisdom is the perfect balance and beauty of you and of the universe that it relates to. When you're disconnected from the power, the energy, the blissfully innate part of yourself, the expression of Moxie, you've lost the person you were meant to be.

> *If you don't stand for something,*
> *you'll fall for anything.*

How does this happen, you ask? Simply put, the learned traits that the brain is fed and saves up over the years become involuntary, much like blinking, swallowing, heartbeats and the like. Influencers who are also governed by their own Inner Critics have nurtured the egoistic self, the Inner Critic. She automatically calls and pulls you back whenever you dare to venture away from the grounded behaviors she sees as predictable, comprehendible and above all, Safe.

Where **Nature** says, "Be yourself, you're different, you'll shine and change the world around you just by using what I gave you," **Nurture** says, "Hold on, just one cotton-pickin' minute! There's a big world out there, and you have to fit in and self protect if you're to survive. Let's just toss a few bumpers and blinders on you before you get hurt."

Nature = Inner Being = True Self
Nurture = Inner Critic = False Self

Don't go throwing flaming daggers just yet. Your Inner Critic means well. She helped you cope and create meaning out of your early childhood experiences. She kept you safe. You may not have gotten through some of the hard times without her. Your real challenge is to discern which voice is hers and which one is your true un-conditioned voice. It's your choice to either obey her outdated warnings or stick a sock in her mouth when it comes time for action. Don't panic; you'll learn to recognize her voice as different from that of your True Self. You'll understand why she's always there in your ear and how to ease her constant need to keep you safe, sound and in the same exact place.

Let's say you want to get out of the work-a-day rat race and build your own business empire. You're longing, you're torn, because you have kids, a full time job, no start-up capital and everyone you know already thinks you're a bit flakey or warns you of the risk. Your True Self knows you're a free spirit, loves that about you and delights in the inspiration, wonderment and glee you feel every time you imagine yourself on the cover of *Forbes* or *O Magazine*.

Your True Self says, "You can! Take a risk; I believe in you! As you start out—perhaps with a website and a little marketing—the positive energy and excitement you feel will boost you to a higher level at work, at home, inside. If mama ain't happy, ain't nobody happy, and I really want to see you smile again. This is who you are... Do it!"

Meanwhile, grumbling about in her dark little cave, your Inner Critic is listening to the nonsense and doesn't at all like what she's hearing. She wanders out with her tattered old umbrella, waiting for the rain that's sure to come, blocking the sunshine so she won't be late to the inevitable storm.

"And just how in the hell do you think that's gonna work, huh?" she objects. "What, you got boulders for brains? Your daughter needs shoes. Your son needs karate lessons. And really, can you possibly compete with everyone else out there? You've got responsibilities. This is no time for more of your classic, self-indulgent dreaming. Besides, if you can even get some clients, you'd be a real jerk if you worked long hours to grow the business instead of spending time with your family! That marketing money is eating into the down payment for a new house. What about that college education you promised your kid? Once you spend it, it's gone. That's it. Then what'll you do, genius? Stare at the website of your business that tanked after you tuck your kiddos into the back seat of the car you live in?"

> *"A dynamic struggle goes on within a person between what she or he consciously thinks on the one hand, and on the other, some insight, some perspective that is struggling to be born." - Rollo May*

So, who wins? Whose voice is stronger, louder? How in touch are you with both sides of your psyche? There's one way to know for sure who wears the pants in your brain: did you get your business up, running, turning a juicy profit? Did you ever quit that day job or did you turn your desire into a time-consuming money-sucking hobby? How often does the idea, the instinct, the drive to see your name up in lights come flooding back in? Once a day, once a week… every time your life feels overwhelming and you've had too much?

And, if you haven't pursued your dream, are all of the things your bratty Inner Critic said true? Would you have compromised the stability of your family's lives by confidently taking a risk, believing in your ability to succeed? Does that make you a bad parent? If so, whose standards are you leaning on in order to beat yourself up? Are you of much use to them in your current worn down state, and wouldn't they revel in seeing you refreshed, charged, Happy? Would you really have denied your child a future so you could have what you wanted? No, being the shining example of an authentic life well lived is the greatest gift you can give to your child, to others and especially to yourself.

You can put almost any thought, dream or want into the same context, and the questions you ask yourself will render the same conclusion. I wanted to dance. I had the lines, the drive and that beautiful inner fire that inspired everyone who watched me. I was a great dancer. So are you…whatever is your "dance" in life.

Nature said, "This is where you belong, in the perfect marriage between body and mind. Use what I gave you and you will succeed."

Nurture said, "It's a long, hard road. Most people fail. Then what? Look how hard the road is on you now; you can't even keep your head up. Besides, if you aren't good enough, and you're probably not, the world will toss you to the ground. Be an employee; don't go for the executive position or the entrepreneurial venture. That's safe. No surprises."

You learn, through the process of getting out of your own way, that life is all about destinations, navigation and attitude. You are the energy that you send out there, and you are the efforts that you give. We bring in what we emit, we get what we give and what we hold true in our beliefs and we go in exactly the direction we're pointing. I was pointing toward getting through today so I could decide what I wanted to be when I grew up, on my own time, waiting for answers to fall into my lap.

The problem with aiming your arrow toward just getting through today is that the next day is just another day like today. Likewise, the downfall of allowing your Inner Critic to point your arrow in the wrong direction, or (yikes!) not at all, is that you'll go exactly to that place. And that place is exactly the wrong place for someone as special as you are.

CHAPTER FOUR

YOU'RE NOT GOOD ENOUGH!

> *"Slumps are like a soft bed. They're easy to get into and hard to get out of."*
> *- Johnny Bench*

You hope things will change. Oh, yeah. We all know what that means. Wish in one hand, despair in the other. Tossing money into fountains... wishing on falling stars. Dorothy leaning on a rusty tractor singing wishes to a rainbow. Wishing you'd done things differently. Wishing this person or that person would come around to your way of thinking. Wishing you were prettier, wishing you were born in another era. Land sakes alive, people! You're excellence in motion! Embrace your magnificence and step into it so you become the very thing you hold in your dreams.

Yet most people wish for someone else or some other thing to come along and pull them out of the slump or "fix" their sorry ass.

Well, guess what? You are not now nor were you ever broken. You've just bought into your Inner Critic cow patties and are stuck in fear, fight, flee or freeze.

Wishers aren't doers. Wishers can't see what's been inside of them all along. And since you weren't lucky enough to be whacked in the head by a flying window during a tornado and to dream up the fantastical truth about life and who you are, we'll have to start from square one. So just who the hell are you, anyway?

> *"Be who you are and say what you feel. Those who mind don't matter, and those who matter don't mind." - Dr. Seuss*

You are the creator of all that you experience. This is a clear, true, innate and undeniable fact. You create the good stuff and you create the bad stuff. When you're whipping up delicious banquets of outcomes, you capture motion, light, sound, beauty, presence and emotion in everything you do. Maybe your strengths lie in words. Do you move and touch people with your innovations or your heart-felt service? Perhaps it's your abilities with animals, or the way others relate to and trust you. Whatever the draw is that you have on the universe, your True Self is the one responsible for taking you there. The calm, clear, exciting voice that beckons from the pit of your gut, prompting you out of fear and indecision, begging you to go forth and create.

Wishes and un-acted upon dreams are merely your True Self politely reminding you that you're not where you should be, and that you aren't doing what nature meant for you in the beginning. The ways you allow yourself to feel trapped, crowded, controlled, manipulated and herded like so many cattle in a stampede to the top are not natural. These are nurtured, inherited behaviors and ways of thinking that defeat your motivation and smother your creativity. Madness, I tell you. Sheer madness!

This is the beginning of a beautiful, riveting journey for you, and one that you were meant to take. All along, no matter where you have gone, whom you have associated yourself with, or what you have done to survive, there was an internal warmth and assuredness that you either couldn't hear or unwittingly ignored. That calm excitement at the pit of your gut is the caring, intelligent guide who will see that you reach your many destinations. It is there to call on whenever you're feeling stuck or uninspired.

Your True Self has been right there all along, through every pain, dream, setback and self-defeating decision you've ever made, and she's been begging you to reconsider! It's my privilege to help you identify, understand and listen for your True Self and to let her lead you out of the stuckness, musts, have-to's and not-enough's of a forced and should-be life.

Okay, first things first. Don't be afraid to get kooky and silly with your endeavors and experiences, because taking ourselves too seriously is draining, exhausting and downright boring. Who says learning and growing have to be hard and meticulous? The truth is, everything you'll find in this book is already within you to be revealed. All of it is yours to reclaim. It's just been drowned and talked out of you over the years of stress, survival and pessimism.

> *"Anyone who has never made a mistake*
> *has never tried anything new."*
> *- Albert Einstein*

You can't get back those years, and why would you even want to? Look at all you've learned and everything you've seen along the way. The lessons you learn without trying are the ones that often mean the most. You're still here, right now, and that means that every second hereafter will find you a little bit wiser and better off from the one before. So, without cursing or pining away for past fates, do as the True Self does, and zealously get on with it already!

Okay, so in the beginning, when you were a child, you saw the world and your future in vivid bright splashes of color. Everything was a new adventure, and you just knew there was something calling to you out there in that big ol' world. Your spirits were hard to dash, and you had little fear of what was on the other side of that door.

You had heroes, because you saw something in your favorite people and characters that mimicked the inner callings of your own spirit. You had Moxie! You expressed a True Self who was strong and powerful and beckoned you not only to dream, but also to boldly test the boundaries that were set up around you. Discover! Climb! Learn! Laugh! Yes! Go There! Do That! Limits?... there's No Such Thing!

> *"If you are going to doubt something, doubt your limits!" - Don Ward*

You created the world around you when you were young, or at least you tried really hard to. But, as with all good things, the "real world" and the adults who were charged with your care could only let the happy-go-lucky, whimsical, lackadaisical, fairyland attitude go until you were five or six. And then came time for matriculation, conditioning and preparation for the "normal" life that you would surely inherit. Not so suddenly you became clone-like, even if you didn't realize it was happening. Individualism was trained out of you, uniqueness became something to feel ashamed of and standing out in the crowd became a punishable offense.

Any variance from "normal", "controlled" behavior at school or at home was looked upon as a nuisance—inconvenient and inciting rebellion. Harmless, natural, unencumbered curiosity and energy became things of annoyance and were aggressively countered. Your True Self is delightfully mischievous and playful for a reason, though… she finds beauty, wisdom, humor and inspiration in every innocent pleasure you conjure. She's guarding and paving the road to individuality for you.

As life progressed, those around you who were "smarter and wiser" influenced how you molded and adopted your thoughts, actions, goals and everyday behaviors. Guided by the principals and smothering tactics they had experienced throughout life, they wanted to protect you, they wanted to do right by you and they didn't want you to stray into a life they couldn't understand. The Inner Critic in them, their self-doubt and fears, was going to get through to you, shape you into something reliable and before you knew it you were confused, disillusioned, lonely and you just wanted to break free from all the regulations and calls to normalcy.

After all the frustration and damage, you struck out on your own to have fun because you were tired of being told what to do and how to do it. Once this was done, though, and the time for survival was upon you, the stronger part of your subconscious took over. Was the more prominent voice in you the Inner Critic, nurtured and structured by the safe, conventional ways that were pounded into you as a youngster? Or did you center yourself in your dreams—pointing toward where your True Self, the keeper of your Moxie, was tugging—and hold on for the wild, exciting, uncertain but certainly worthwhile ride that you deserved?

> *"To me, the main thing about living on the planet is to know who the hell you are, and be real about it. That's the reason I'm still alive."*
> *- Keith Richards*

Even if you did pursue your dreams and ambitions, did you do so in the spirit of personal freedom, devotion and inner success, or did you just want to prove them all wrong and be right? One is positive energy that easily regenerates. The other is negative energy that eventually destroys.

You have to watch out for the forked tongue of that cowardly old fart, because she works against your True Self so efficiently that it can be hard to tell who's doing the talking.

Perhaps we should get a closer look at the Inner Critic, shall we? Now, granted, she may have saved your butt from time to time… she's the voice of fear, safety, must, have to and practicality. She means to keep you in line with the majority of the other humans battering around in the rat race of survival, and she's rather good at taking the wind out of your sails.

"Oh," she grunts and grumbles, "you got all the excess energy and time, huh? If you Really want to accomplish something, why don't you figure out how in the hell to pay the credit card balance or where your next gas-guzzling car is coming from? How about that D your kid got in algebra? If you want to dig into something, there's your list!"

She speaks to us as our elders, superiors and caregivers have in the past. "Focus! Feet on the Ground! Head out of the clouds! Don't draw attention to yourself! You wanna be different? Just what we need, more trouble and inconvenience! Get back to work; your real job won't do itself!"

The important thing to remember about your life and the way you go forward from here is that every great thing came from one person, one vision, one little flicker of imagination and creativity. You worry so much about marketability, then you hem and haw about not pleasing everyone. What you're missing is the voice of your heart, your True Self, who owns and expresses your Moxie—that courageous confidence to relentlessly pursue your burning desires.

The authentic part of you is telling you that whatever You give of You is Your gift to give, and those who are genuinely drawn in by the honesty and uniqueness of your creations will take notice, because their own intuition and creativity are sparked by the greatness of what yours did. That is how you become successful. Merely by finishing what you started, no matter how many times you have to start over, no matter how many times you feel you have failed and by following your own rules. Better yet, No Rules! You have to replace Rules with Authenticity. Rules are like kryptonite to imagination and individuality. Rules are applied to society as a means of safety, peace, order and control. You don't need any of those things to create.

> *"When love and skill work together, expect a masterpiece." - John Ruskin*

Some call it their inner eye, their intuition, their talent; their instinct… by any name, the heart-centered essence is that all-knowing, all-seeing brightness that points you toward the callings and trueness of your natural life. Though it's always there, and always has been, most are not guided by it. Maybe you can hear it or feel it, and at times it nudges and elbows at you constantly to the point of craziness. But, you still aren't obeying that cool, confident, instinctive voice... you're still not pointing your life, your works and your mind in the right direction.

> *"The intuitive mind is a sacred gift and the rational mind is a faithful servant. We have created a society which honors the servant and has forgotten the gift." - Albert Einstein*

Which direction is the right one? The direction that feels good even when everything's a mess. The direction that lets you look up for a change and take stock in yourself rather than in the "important, meaningful, real" work that you do for someone else's profit. Of course, I'm not suggesting you walk away from a career that helps support your family in your desired lifestyle and start selling folded paper stork hats on the street corner... unless that's what really calls to you.

You're a brilliant creator. We all are. Learn to listen for, converse with and trust in the callings of your True Self. Begin to arm yourself against the Inner Critic who'll rise up again and again to pop your bubbles and block your sun. Start putting your long strangled dreams, visions, ambitions and talents back where they belong—at the forefront of your life.

A friend of mine calls it writer's block. Some call it blank canvas syndrome or analysis paralysis, while others won't admit to the frustration and embarrassment they feel when inspiration seems to elude them. As creative beings, we're expected to bring inspiration and great vision to others in our unique way... and it can be pretty easy to beat up on ourselves when nothing trickles out of us, no matter how much wringing we do. Really? Nothing? I know, sometimes it feels that way. You need to trust and understand, though, that you're never empty.

It's physically and mentally impossible. There are ideas, sounds, shapes, colors and words that sparkle like diamonds waiting to be unearthed. Are you sure there's nothing inside or out to build from, or are you allowing the Inner Critic to tell you that your inspirations are not good enough, not deep or provocative enough, not worth the trouble? Yup. I went there.

I went there because I've been there. The freedom we feel as creators of unique and original ideas is such an immense privilege and is a refreshing, beautiful ability that needs to be exercised, cared for, replenished and rested. Your gift is almost like a muscle. If you use it often, expanding and contracting it every day, and take it easy when it's tired, it will stay strong and trusty and will sustain you for a very long time.

If you don't use it enough, it may work, but it hurts for a while each time you do and lacks the stamina it needs to function correctly. If you force it, and allow it to be manipulated by negative, unnatural sources — an Inner Critic, yours or someone else's—bawling it out, putting it down or cracking the whip, it won't reach its full potential.

You don't always have to be Impressive and Productive. If you place the same type of timing pressures and performance expectations on yourself as the micromanager control freak boss does when you leave early in the evening to have a life, what are you doing to the freedom and untamed expression your gifts afford you? You're killing them, that's what.

You have to be wary of what you expect from yourself, because if the Inner Critic has her way, she'll needle, poke and prod at your every thought, talking you out of some of those key moments and ideas which could be just the juice you need. How can you take away her power, disarm her voice when she has no good argument? How can you stop letting her pressure you, halt her putting limits and rules on your creative processes?

The truth is, forced work feels forced to the creator, the viewer, the reader and the recipients of the end result. Who can force inspiration? You may be able to find it in the strangest places; you may be able to borrow it from a mischievous child; it may hit you like a ton of bricks while you sip a beer and swipe the cat's tail out of your face. But it won't come to you until you let go, lay loose and let your True Self have the reins.

CHAPTER FIVE

YOU'RE STUCK!

> *"It is not because things are difficult that we do not dare, it is because we do not dare that they are difficult."* - Seneca

Maybe it's better to have the same experiences, even the really shitty ones, than to venture into the unknown. At least you know what you're getting into and that you'll survive it. Probably much safer to toil away quietly and privately in the little corner you've etched out for yourself than to risk the possible humiliation and aggravation of being judged and misunderstood.

Why not keep those dreams and visions to yourself, never be face to face with a critic who, in your mind, could make or break your entire future. A critic who would mirror the inner nagging of your very own ego self, Your Inner Critic, proving her right and shutting down your dreams. Boy, that Inner Critic is a real bugger. Bad enough to be criticized by others—you have your own Inner Critic to bad-mouth you when nobody else is around.

You see, by Creating illusions, or allowing your Inner Critic to do so, and believing in these falsehoods more fervently than you believe in yourself, you're able to hide from that which you think you don't know.

It takes a lot of trust to hold your vision out in front of others and ask them to believe in you. But what matters more, and what makes all of the fear and self-denial fall to the wayside, is integrity. Personal integrity. Standing firmly, powerfully, centered in the truth of who you are, the unique passions that drive you and all that you value, beginning with yourself. No other person, thing or event can make or break you, tell you you're wrong or not good enough. Only You Can Invalidate You.

> *"Most men lead lives of quiet desperation, and go to the grave with the song still within them."*
> *- Henry David Thoreau*

You've already experienced the pain of self-inflicted invalidation. You think that if you stay small and hold back your authentic expression— your Moxie—you can hide from and avoid another layer of hurt. You fear that you'll simply crumble into a million pieces if you suffer any more internal pain. The fear of using your Moxie—your full authentic self-expression and awareness—is the deepest and most stunting form of resistance you face.

Resistance. E-Gads! What a largely underrated source of discontent and confusion. It shows up throughout your life in the form of procrastination and F.E.A.R. (finding excuses and reasons) telling you why you can't do, have and be what you really long for most.

In order for you to understand and rectify those things that you either stubbornly resist or refuse to resist, there are some basic principals of resistance for you to understand so you realize why your resistance hurts so good. Yes, I said good. You wouldn't resist if you weren't getting something out of resisting.

One of your very first stumbling blocks on the road is that you will Resist what you know will help you move into bigger and better opportunities. Who knows if you'll be able to handle it? What if you fail? What if you look like a fool? So you'd rather suffer through another unsatisfying and unfulfilling day than venture out into the unknown. Where you are right now is what you know! The Inner Critic Law clearly states: "Knowing = Safety. Safety = Easy. Easy = Smart. Smart = Knowing Your Place. Repeat Cycle Until Life Over."

The Inner Critic has done her job. She's kept you safe and sound your entire life. (Her version of safety, anyhow.) She's not at all concerned with whether or not you lived a fulfilling or purposeful life. Whether or not you've experienced any joy or satisfaction is a moot point for her. Your happiness is irrelevant. Safety is the only thing that matters. Sort of like Gollum in Lord of the Rings… he doesn't care about anything other than that confounding ring. And just look at how enslaved he was by his tormented pursuit!

> *"Have the courage to take your own thoughts seriously, for they will shape you."*
> *- Albert Einstein*

The Inner Critic serves up steady self-denial rather than consistent progress. It's not in any way rewarding, and it doesn't get you to a better place, but it insures that the little hole you've carved out for yourself will still be there for you to hide in tomorrow morning. Resistance to your life goals is not futile—quite the contrary. Resistance is a powerful way of saying, "I can live with the Devil I know already, and I'm used to her holding me back. At least I don't have to venture out into unknown territory where others can cause me pain through judgment and criticism."

And so you put off your dreams, exchange them for safer desires, or worse yet, the dreams of well meaning yet misguided influencers. You live your life pleasing the people around you, living in a way that supports and validates them and their dreams instead of your own. And it hurts. It doesn't feel good. Yet, it's safe. Safety is what you get for staying small. You get to stay safe… crawling well below the radar of what is your greater purpose. It never occurs to you that out on the limb, where all the fruit is, is also safe. What's more, stepping out on that limb so you can taste the sweet fruit that nature provided just for you Feels Good!

But you don't know what it would be like to wake up each morning feeling Good, looking forward to how you can expand your possibilities for the new and glorious day. Better put off the new endeavor until tomorrow. Not ready! Not ready! Stay right where you are. Crawl back underneath your covers of limited thinking and narrow, groggy vision.

How many additional things will conveniently become more important to you and those you surround yourself with two tomorrows from now? Three? Thirty? I'll just bet that if you don't even try that hard, you can Always find something more pressing, more urgent, more "productive," more important to do than that which calls to you. Why? Because you're afraid of yourself. You're afraid that you'll wake up one day successful, and you won't know who you are or what to do.

What would life be like without the constant pressures, the delusions of mediocrity and negativity, to guide your every waking emotion? If the grueling schedule and the horrid problems that keep you running ragged each day were no longer the driving force behind your actions, what would you do? If you became someone who actually loved her life experience, you would then be a round peg trying to fit into a square hole.

Your experiences would no longer "fit in" to your definition and expectations of what life is all about. What would you then have to do to gain a place in the world, to relate to people, to be "normal" again? This is where the Inner Critic tosses some more self-sabotage your way, forcing you back into your "rightful" place.

Some people misguidedly think that in order for a new life to emerge, the old one has to end. Bollocks! However, ending the life that you know, the only one you've ever experienced, is what you fear the most. You don't want to be someone else, you don't want to have to find new ways to talk and act and Be. You're frightened by the life you envision as rightfully yours because you separate the conditioned, suppressed you that you live as now from the natural, authentic you. With all of that passion and talent, your purpose in life is to express your magnificent full potential. However, you think that in order to deserve the life your heart, your gut instinct, knows to be your birthright, you have to lose who you are and become someone else. Someone better, yet worse. Someone unrecognizable to you and the people you know.

Not True! Your True Self has been right there with you all along. You're no stranger to the being who seeks truth, light, inspiration and wonderment. You've shown up as your authentic self in all of those "in the zone" moments, when you're joyously and wholeheartedly engaged in what you love to do. Those times when you're completely unaware of time or outside pressures.

You don't remember the last time you took a breath or felt hungry, because your physical body is merely a tool you're using to help you actualize your vision. You're totally in the present moment, focused and fully available to whatever comes next... no questions or second thoughts about colors, inspirations, proper prose. You felt Fabulous! You felt fabulous because you were you, and you showed up as the Real, Authentic You that nature created.

You aren't meant to place yourself into a new life that doesn't belong to you. You are meant to Moxie Up! Shed those attachments and ways of thinking that keep you disconnected from your rightful authentic life. Like peeling an onion, you remove the conditioned, unnatural parts of yourself so your natural beauty and gifts can expand, blossoming boldly into the world. You're no longer hidden. You're no longer hiding. You're present, standing centered in the truth of who you are. And you're beautiful.

> **YOU HAVE THE CONFIDENT COURAGE TO ACHIEVE AUTHENTIC GREATNESS WITH UNRELENTING DRIVE AND PASSION.**

Why is it that your Inner Critic thinks those more "fortunate" than you are as#&oles, and that you aren't even good enough to stand beside them? Because she's a confused and frightened old fart who hates change! Any change. Even positive change. She doesn't have a valid reason. All the Inner Critic knows is that she'd better give you a reason Not to want what They have, or the next thing you know you will change and become one of Them! Your Inner Critic doesn't know how to live within the richness in color of an abundant life. Black and white, and perhaps a little beige, will do just fine (thank you very much!).

In order to make you feel better about the same rich lifestyle, she beats up on the people who enjoy what you don't have. Your Inner Critic doesn't know how to serve up anything else. Negativity is familiar and comforting to the Inner Critic. It's the easiest way of blaming everything and everyone around for the discontent and anger she feels.

> *"Whether you think you can or think you can't,*
> *you're right." - Henry Ford*

She's protecting you by telling you it's not your fault when fault, or any other form of judgment, has nothing to do with taking responsibility for your life. Being responsible for your life means owning all of your life experiences, good and bad, and knowing that You are the all-powerful being who creates all of it. And as the profound creator, you can learn how to create more of the good and less of the bad as you journey confidently along.

Examine your experiences, past and present. Reveal the embedded lesson, the message that life is sending you out of the experience. There's no room at the examination table for Inner Critic judgment and ridicule, so kindly show her to the waiting room, gag her mouth with duct tape (the magical adherent that works for Everything) and focus on the wonderful opportunities that every experience has to offer.

Resistance is saying NO to who you are. Too scared to express your Moxie. Fear of putting your naked authentic self out there to possibly be rejected is what holds you back. Period. Your Inner Critic has explained to you how pathetic starving entrepreneurs are, how rude and obnoxious movie stars are, how fickle and judgmental skinny people are, how snobby and jerky rich people are, how snooty and eccentric artists are, how annoying and belittling "happy" people are.

She's been trying to convince you that you don't want what they have. You've been listening to and gauging your life choices around these preconceived and contrived notions for Years and Years. You think you don't want to become the person that your misguided ego self turns green over with jealousy. You fight it tooth and nail, from the very onset of all of your choices, and even more so through the important choices you fail to make at all.

Okay, just take a deep breath and chill out for a minute. Though this all seems overwhelming and a bit too heavy, the steps you'll take to unravel the ball of self-denial are quite a bit simpler. Your first step will be to recognize the voice of your True Self. Her voice is the Exact Opposite of all of the begrudging and resistant behavior.

Hers is calm and steady, confident and enthralled with life and all of the possibilities waiting for you. She's there when you're motivated to create, when you come up with that grand vision for your next endeavor, when you dream of changing the world with your visions and the masterpieces you produce. She points toward success and authenticity at all times and never wavers or pouts. She doesn't compete. She never judges, you or anybody else. She doesn't get caught up in thoughts of money or fame. She's all about Moxie, boldly expressing YOU, the Real You. She'll always show you what you need to see in order to claim your place in your own life.

Your True Self lets you know that you're saying NO to your authentic life through a deep feeling of sadness and desperation.

Know this: What you resist the most is what you, your True Self, is calling for you to become. If you take on what you resist, your life and emotional outlook will change in miraculous ways.

> "_If you limit yourself only to what seems possible or reasonable, you disconnect yourself from what you truly want, and all that is left is a compromise._" - Robert Fritz

For example, if you fear public speaking, get out there and talk in front of people as often as you can. A board meeting, a charity fundraiser, open mic night at the local watering hole. Even if you stand there, mute, petrified, with the classic deer in the headlights syndrome dripping from your every pore, you'll have faced your fear head on. You've got an extremely entertaining story to tell at least, and at best you're one step closer to conquering your fear. With a little time, the story won't be the devastating experience you always thought it would be. It will be a story you tell while you lovingly laugh at yourself.

I know this is true because I'm telling you the story, my story, now. I stood there like a frozen zombie (I'm quite sure there wasn't one speck of color in my face), until I rambled for a brief moment about who the heck knows what (I'm quite certain I couldn't even remember where I was, let alone the riveting subject matter), and then nervously giggled and laughed my way down off the podium (A.K.A. the public pinnacle of social death and humiliation), to mixed and merely courteous applause. But, you'll never guess… okay, I'll tell you.

I didn't die. No one shunned me. Nobody really cared at all. Realizing, at long last, that I wouldn't die made it that much easier each subsequent time I took the stage. And I did take the stage, again and again, each time easier than the last. I'm still not the most eloquent, polished or articulate public speaker, but I never shy from the opportunity to speak my truth in front of an audience. *What a rush!*

You measure and judge yourself constantly. (Well, your good old Inner Critic does.) Against what? Why, other people of course. Heroes, Joe-Blows, competitors, associates, old teachers, neighbors, parents, siblings, intellectuals—really everyone. She measures your worth As Compared To the perceived value of other people. The reason this never works? Well, there's no control specimen in the experiment. You're not like anybody else, and nobody else is like you. This is an absolute fact, undeniable, unchangeable. Yet you place your self worth, even your identity, in the hands of others. You allow others, or your perceptions of those around you, to define who you are and what you're worth. Nonsense!

Your True Self recognizes and revels in those who glow with dreams, light, strength and inner beauty, to remind you of who you are. She doesn't compare you against them. She enthusiastically reminds you of your own potential and of the possibilities for your own life. Your Inner Critic does the comparisons, and you'll always be either "Way Better than the person" or "Not good enough to lick the shoes of the person" by her misguided standards. You see, where your heart and deepest inner core invited you to learn, grow and be jovial in the gift of the great and inspiring relationship, your Inner Critic tried to force you to choose: "Her or Me, huh? Who's it gonna be? The half-wit, airy-fairy who's full of wide-eyed inspiration, or me, the one who's always kept you safe?"

If you've been involved with, raised by or lead by a person who's ruled and controlled by their own Inner Critic, you've received these same ultimatums and jabs from them as well. "I'm the know-all, the be-all, the end-all of your entire existence. Do unto Me as I say, or when you fail and land flat on your ass, don't come crying to Me!" The negative voice of the Inner Critic is a universal internal language… it just keeps spreading and breeding and repeating itself until it consumes everything and every one it falls on, as long as it finds an impressionable audience. It's all about control, spurred on by fear of loss, humiliation, misunderstanding and failure.

The people who "should" all over you, telling you who you should be, what you should do and what you should have, really do mean well. Like all of us, they're doing their very best with the only light by which they can see. We mustn't forget that most people are guided by the Inner Critic, and like the Inner Critic, they're only able to view "what's good for you" from the point of safety and protection. So, even though they're trying to help, they're severely misguided. What's good for you is for You to Be You. Without exception!

If you allow yourself to be manipulated and forced into a corner by your own Inner Critic, those who are ruled by their Inner Critics will sniff you out and place you under their thumb. Only the Moxie empowered True Self has the presence, the grace, the strength and the positive determination to free you from whatever binds. Whether it's an abusive relationship, productivity block, weight issues, career woes, blank canvas syndrome, whatever. She sees what you're capable of, she knows what you need to be free and whole and she'll take you there, if you just allow her.

> *"Each relationship you have with another person reflects the relationship you have with yourself." -* *Alice Deville*

How, you say? Well, begin by asking your Inner Being, your Higher Self, your soul or whatever you want to call the core of your inner True Self, what she wants. LISTEN for the answer, as there surely is At Least one answer. Allow the pure, honest voice to remind you of your deepest desires. Calm the monkey mind voice of the Inner Critic so you hear and concentrate from deep within you. Respond by taking one step, even a tiny baby step, toward that direction. Begin to show up in your day, and thus in your life, as a person who has already accomplished the desire. Visualize who you would be, what you would do and what you would have in that life. Have that "I've done it, I Am It" energy with you always.

If your Inner Critic fights back, the dreadfully frightened little weasel, using dastardly ammo such as procrastination, creative block, finding excuses and reasons (F.E.A.R.) or making you want to eFF Everything And Run (F.E.A.R.), visualize the things you (your I.C.) fear the most. Finally finishing your hard-fought novel only to have it misunderstood and underestimated by publisher after publisher? Moving to that magical, tropical island just to starve cause you can't find a J.O.B. (just over broke)? Being denied admission to that prestigious school? Getting rejected for that role you wanted to play because your nose is too big? Hearing "No" a couple of hundred times? Now... ask yourself this: Would you actually die if any of these things came to pass? What would you do to overcome the impact of your decision if it didn't pay off right away? Would you be ashamed of yourself? Would others be ashamed of you? And, most importantly, did you learn anything that will make the next attempt more successful?

What if, from the Inner Critic's standpoint, you put yourself out there and you did indeed fail? Do you believe you're now officially a failure? She told you, she warned you and scolded and threatened and raged, but you did it anyway. "See," she huffs and puffs, "Now What, Genius? We can't go back to the safe, predictable life we had before, because you sacrificed it all for Nothing!"

Your Inner Critic will continue to ream and belittle you—that's all she knows how to do. Perhaps she wants you to do somebody else's work, for a guaranteed paycheck on a precise day every week with no hitches or surprises. She doesn't see the work of your Moxie empowered True Self as "real" or "relevant" because nobody has paid for it or referenced it as in demand if it's something of your own innovation. This folderol is nothing but a raging, endless sea of troubled waters if you ask her. Even if you don't ask, she'll tell you. Over and Over she'll make sure you know how she feels about it.

What she doesn't know is that rejection, in any form, is not failure. Rejection is an opportunity to learn and to grow, to reinforce what's innate within you and teach you how to expand and utilize it. This truly is a gift, one that's only offered to those who are brave and authentic enough to try. You'll never waste any experiences that way, as long as you seek the lesson through the ups and the downs. Really, if you went through all the trouble to live through a bad experience, don't you think you deserve to at least learn something from it? Go back, examine the experience and get the gift of the lesson learned!

As you honor your truth, embracing the gifts along the way, your True Self will cheer you on. "Look at you go!" she praises joyously. "You Did It! I Knew It! You Friggin' Rock! What's Next? Let's get ready for the next big project, flop or fly, come on!" She's not comparing you to anybody. She's not measuring the monetary worth of any of your efforts. She's not worried about wasted time or loss of social status. She's not afraid. She's not intimidated at all. She's got Moxie! In spades.

> *"If you want to increase your success rate, double your failure rate."*
> *- Thomas Watson*

She's energized, inspired, enlightened and ready for your next adventure. "Well, now that we know one more thing that doesn't work, we're getting closer! Yay!" Your True Self knows you by heart. She's been here for you all along, and she's always provided the guidance you needed to turn your dreams into reality. Your True Self knows with certainty that you have the ability to overcome any and all challenges you'll surely face. You're in for the ride of your life, the only one you get to take, and she knows that it's worth every bump and rut in the road.

Are you a passenger in the back seat of a Buick sedan, driven by that grumpy old "hands at 10 & 2" granny who's being passed as if standing still (all the other people are crazy, sick, delinquent, lunatics for doing over 45 on the Freeway—Hooligans!). She's headed to the senior luncheon special at the worst restaurant ever (she's eaten there forever, sees no reason to switch it up now) before leaving a 50 cent tip (that was considered extremely generous when first she dined here, 56 years ago) and heading back for her third (and final) nap of the day (which started at 9 am and will end at 7:30 pm sharp)? This is what life is like when you're a passenger to your Inner Critic. She does what she does; she knows what she knows. And she hasn't changed her pattern since she was knee high to a donkey.

You're just daydreaming in the backseat, the years of your life flying by as quickly as the other cars passing, wondering if the Cornish hen will be frostbitten like it was yesterday. When will you offer to drive? Better yet, when will you just take the keys and assert your new plan? You are, after all, stronger than she is. She's not the boss of you, unless you let her think she is! Yes, the Inner Critic will have to eat sometime, and you'd be more than happy to pay, but why not at the time and place of your choosing? If you continue to empower her, your life will remain as limp, boring and repetitive as it is from the back seat.

Until now, you've primarily acted upon the guidance of that freaked out Inner Critic. It's time to empower your True Self once again to mentor you as you actualize your full potential and create your reality from your dreams. "I'm so excited for you right now, I'm doing my happy dance. Hey, ya wanna join me?" your eager True Self celebrates.

She understands you can't be measured against or by anyone else's visions, standards or accomplishments unless you give your power over to them. Perish The Thought! Your True Self is all about empowering You, and You alone. She loves the world and what it holds for You. And you, leading with Moxie, energized by your True Self, will begin to gain the respect and admiration of not only yourself, but also those around you. You'll be the shining light, that inspiring beacon that reminds everyone else of his or her own possibilities. Even those who are ruled unhappily by their ego selves can't deny the power and spirit of someone who takes action, claims their authenticity and sticks to it no matter how hard it may seem.

> *"Cease trying to work everything out with your minds. It will get you nowhere. Live by intuition and inspiration and let your whole life be Revelation." - Eileen Caddy*

In this way, you've not only freed yourself, but you've begun a chain reaction of positive thinking and forward motion. If you listen for and trust in your True Self, you'll believe in your own unique purpose. And once you believe, everyone who's lucky enough to stand beside your fire will feel his or her own power and inspiration ignite. It really does work this way. I know, because I have the Moxie to be empowered by my own True Self. I've been to and lived many of the inner shadows that haunt you and I know you by Heart. We're all connected, you see.

Start with something very small. Baby steps catch on quickly. You know that if you've had the pleasure of watching a little miracle toddle her way out of the bouncy seat and into the land of adventure. These little wonders start out with an internal call to action, a vision and instinct, the moxie to propel themselves toward the toy that nobody will hand to them. By holding onto anything that will stay still, (and sometimes even irresistible things that won't, like the dog), and inching their little toes clumsily forward, they creep ahead with no knowledge or practice, just a hunger, a goal and some ambition.

Within days of the first effort, they've fallen a time or two, maybe bruised an arm or bumped a head, but they know what they want, and by damn they will have that toy by rights! And, lo and behold, one bright and glorious evening, during a try much like the ones before, they let go of that still or fuzzy thing, throw their legs forward three, four, six times, and the delicious prize lands squarely in their gooey, happy mouths! That's the Moxie driven and expressed True Self.

From there, the pudgy, determined little munchkin knows no boundaries, and within mere heartbeats of her initial triumph, you'll have to check the dryer before you start it, the driveway before you back your car out and the grocery cart before you leave the store. Because, all of a sudden, the little tot is everywhere at once! The world is her playground, she knows no fear, she has no preconceived notions about anyone or anything… she's in it to discover, play and find the places she enjoys most in the world. (No, not "find her place in the world." That kind of talk is for ninnies.)

It's true. I'm saying that the brazen, full of moxie, childhood spirit is the closest physical incarnation of your true self as anything you'll ever experience. Aside from a few common sense guidelines that we follow regarding the physical protection of others, and ourselves, it's the spirit that we must listen for and follow. Listen with all your heart. That's where your inner wisdom, truth and authenticity live. That's where your Moxie is waiting for you to express it fully!

Okay, so we can sum up a few points on the subject that will help you to focus on exactly where your thoughts are coming from, the negative and positive ones, and how to tell if it's best to act upon them.

Are you standing in judgment?

Whether of yourself or of someone else, judgment is detrimental to your progress. Judgment means you're resisting a lesson, a tool, a person, an experience or an opportunity that could greatly ease your journey. Any "You Suck!" moments you have, toward yourself or anyone else, are the results of your Inner Critic having a tantrum because she doesn't want to take a single step forward. Nope, not gonna do it. Tell her to friggin' relax, already. While her panties are in a bunch between her cheeks, she could be picking up some extremely helpful hints about where to go next, and how to get there.

Are you good at **F**inding **E**xcuses **A**nd **R**easons?

Do you want to **F#%k** **E**verything **A**nd **R**un?

FEAR.

When you discover that you're coming up with excuses to avoid or run away from something, know that you're in a state of fear. You're resisting the very thing your heart is calling you to do. I resisted public speaking most of my life. I was brilliant at getting out of anything that would require me to speak in front of an audience of more than three people. When I finally got out of my own way of my resistance, I discovered something amazing. I have a lot of fun speaking to groups of people! Oh, I've had that deer-in-the-headlights look a few times on stage and forgotten half of what I wanted to say. No one was the wiser. I just stayed focused in the present moment and words flowed through me. No one in the audience had a clue I blanked out on what I had planned to say, but my True Self shone through.

As my 10-year-old niece tells her friends who are too scared to taste new foods, "Try it! You're not gonna die!" Will everything you know whither away into oblivion if you push it off until you friggin' feel like it? What has to happen before you'll allow yourself to friggin' feel like it? What place does F.E.A.R. have in your life if you're no longer afraid of it? Being fearless takes a little practice, as with everything worthwhile, but Watch Out World once you've mastered the skill. Truth is, you were born masterfully skilled at leading a fearless life. You very quickly forgot that you had the tool the moment someone yelled "No" or "Don't" at you, and it was buried further and further down each time you were reprimanded for going against the direction of someone else's Inner Critic. The stronger your Inner Critic became, nurtured and fed through self-reinforcement, the more detached you became from your unique and natural power.

Are you Should-ing all over yourself?

If you're having one of those days when much of your time is spent beating up on yourself or your circumstance, just sit on that pity pot of yours. Stink up the place. When you're done, flush. Reach for a new perspective. One with the Moxie to empower you to think, speak and act in alignment with who you really are and what you really want.

To do that, consider, maybe, Not Should-ing All Over Yourself in the first place! This is another example of your Inner Critic pitting you against and comparing you with Other People. Remember, there's no control specimen in the adventure known as life. The sooner you realize that all of your goals and ambitions are best served Within You, the more quickly and happily you'll be on your way.

Your beauty and strength are Immeasurable! Unique! Vibrant! Authentic! You've got Moxie! You are You! Who could ask for anything more? You decide what's important, worthwhile, what's a priority and what's not. If you want to lose weight because the skinny girl across the street makes you feel bad, you'll be Should-ing all over yourself for the rest of your life, because you're never gonna look like her. It's not physically possible for you to ever look like that person.

So if looking "that way, like her" is the driving force behind your actions, you have no attainable goal to reach. See? But, if you decide that You want to be healthier, and that You want to know what it would feel like and be like to see Yourself as healthy as possible, now that's a goal worth setting. Attainable? Absolutely! For your own reasons, not for the should-do or be and supposed-to advice from anyone else, including your Inner Critic.

Apply that to anyone you admire—your favorite artist, corporate leader, writer, rock star—and you have the same answer. *Have the Moxie to Be You!* It's the only truly attainable thing You can be. Be inspired by the strengths that those you admire showed in attaining their goals, and then go forth and forge your own path. The kicker: Nobody else will ever be able to be You, either. They get to be Them. How wonderful!

> *"When you feel in your gut who you are and then dynamically pursue it – don't give up and don't back down – you're going to mystify a lot of folks."*
> *- Bob Dylan*

You are here to mystify a lot of folks!

(I know, I already said this. It's worth repeating. Again and again. Write it on several post-it notes and stick them everywhere to remind yourself of your true purpose.)

CHAPTER SIX

YOU'RE A FAILURE!

> *"I don't know the key to success, but the key to failure is trying to please everybody."* – *Bill Cosby*

And therein lies the truth of all matters. There's only one person you can be completely true to, and you're stuck with that person for the rest of your life. You can't escape yourself, and you have to answer to yourself before you answer to or for anyone else. Who will think the same as you do, or care as much about the same things? Who has the most to gain or lose based on the choices you make or the experiences you conjure up along the way? This can be a judicious world, and as such always seems quicker to blame than it is to credit, so you may as well get used to being your own best advocate. Face it… you're nothing without You.

And that brings me to the way you think everyone else on the planet perceives you. Not that it should matter all too much to you, but the way others see and relate to you has a lot to do with your self-esteem and confidence—the way you see yourself. You may worry as an entrepreneur that you aren't good enough, that your work will be misunderstood and under-appreciated and that you'll struggle for years before anyone will be generous enough to give you that big break.

> *"Whenever two people meet, there are actually six people present. There is each man as he sees himself, each man as the other person sees him, and each man as he really is." - James Williams*

That way of thinking is generated and perpetuated by the Inner Critic, who fights tooth and nail to keep you safe from rejection, loss and insecurities. We pull into our experiences what we put out there, so the more judgmental you are of yourself and others, the more judgment and potential ridicule you open yourself up to receiving. Being led by the Inner Critic will draw negativity in like a magnet, and you'll always find reasons to support your Inner Critic's theories about why you suck.

Wrong color, You Suck! Bad call, You Suck! Where the hell did you pick up that lame idea? You Suck! My inspiration lied! My instinct Sucks! Bad timing, poor materials, wrong plan, crappy moods, loss for words... your Inner Critic will always find ways to cut you down before some-body else has a chance to. That way, grumbles the frightened, crotchety Inner Critic, it hurts much less when other critics let loose on you and your work. This way of thinking causes a deep, frozen fear you may not recognize or acknowledge. It kills the genius and beauty of your future undertakings before they even have a chance to bud, let alone bloom.

> *"A new idea is delicate. It can be killed by a sneer or a yawn. It can be stabbed to death by a quip and worried to death by a frown on the right man's brow." - Charles Brower*

In this way, your Inner Critic may have etched you out a life of excuses, amidst "overbearing outside forces", which keep you from running full bang into the center of your true enthusiasm and happiness. You begin to focus on the lies and the criticisms which give you the leverage you need to remain stationary, to stay neutral and to be mediocre. When somebody does see a glimmer of the talent and innate wisdom in you, it's thrilling and encouraging, and you feel alight with ecstatic, dreamy hopes and ambitions.

As soon as you allow your Inner Critic to grab hold of you, however, you crash back into that negative spin where everything has its excuse and its shortcoming. "You Suck! She Lied! (She's your pontificating Inner Critic.) What you want won't come easy this time; it must be a cosmic joke! Everyone will laugh... you may as well chuck it out the window and give it up." Your Inner Critic is woefully misguided, and negative statements, yours and "theirs", empower her to take over what she can, rein you back in and give you plenty of cause to shrivel back up into the safe little station she's carved out for you.

> *"Every man, through fear, mugs his*
> *aspirations a dozen times a day."*
> *- Brendan Francis*

Ah... resentment. It wears so many faces, and serves so many purposes in an unfulfilled "have to" life. If only he'd been different, I could be happy now. If only that person hadn't done that one thing, I probably would've been on cloud nine years ago. If I can make the person feel guilty and remorseful for that one time they took the thing from me, I could find the strength to carry on with my dreams now. This or that person is making my life hard right now; maybe if I guilt them enough they'll make me happier, and then I could forge ahead with the callings of my True Self. Maybe if all the Needy, Clingy, Controlling people in my life would just Back Off and Give a little for a change, maybe I could find my true happiness and calling.

Do you see how easy it is to give power over, good and bad, to anyone besides the one who can actually physically, mentally, spiritually change your circumstances? Don't look over your shoulder or above your head in wonderment... I'm talking to you.

Giving over your entire life to the whims, negative grudges, expectations and demands of other people is something that's nurtured into you from the time you learn to walk. It's so much easier to flow with the current than it is to veer off in your own direction. Your Inner Critic recognizes the easy, paved road, and will call you back onto it at every turn in an attempt to keep from getting lost. In order to keep pace with the rest of the traffic on the road, you're forced to accept things you shouldn't, behave in ways you wouldn't, do things you don't trust or believe in and move along with the flow to avoid being trampled.

It's never too late to step off the highway of the masses onto that little dirt path you've been eyeballing. This is a place where you can look back safely, without being bumped, jarred or blamed, and take a deep breath that you don't have to share with anybody. This is where all the other voices fall away, and you can start learning how to be You again. Have the Moxie to be the Real You, the Worthy, Intuitive, Zealous, Authentic, Responsible and Deliberate person you are at your deepest core.

> *"You will do foolish things, but do them with enthusiasm." - Colette*

The differences between you and those you admire may seem staggering in numbers. Not true. There's only one difference: they have the Moxie to honor and focus upon their True Self. To the extent that you're not happy with yourself and/or lot in life is the extent to which you've lost sight of your True Self, let go of your Moxie and have become the expression of your Inner Critic.

Those who think, speak and act with the Moxie to be, do and have what their heart longs for, took on the responsibility each day to master every opportunity. They never showed up as the victim to anyone or anything, especially their Inner Critic. Extraordinary people have the guts, the confidence and the drive—the Moxie—to show up in life authentically and express their full potential. They remained loyal to their Nature, the True Self, without whom anything new, fresh, exciting or original could ever be done. That's how.

It takes talent, inner focus and stick-to-it-iveness to stay that original, that enthralled and that inspired for so many years. The type of fortitude and unfailing guidance can't be learned or adopted. You already have it within you. It's up to you to bring it forth. Where you see obstacles, have the Moxie to reach for new perspectives.

All of your memories and hardheaded habits are based on your perceptions of past events and the importance you give to them. So, many of the meanings you attached to the events simply must be changed and looked at from a different perspective if you're to get on in another direction. If you keep doing what you do, you keep getting what you get.

Those who make success in their craft look easy and effortless are those who are led bravely and playfully by their bold authentic Moxie. It may not always be easy for your idols and mentors, and it's especially difficult for those creative icons who suffer depression and life-long struggles. Billy Joel, Amy Tan, Jim Carrey and Loraine Bracco are a few among the many celebrities who manage to muster up their Moxie and beauty even in the dismal perceived reality of their emotional conditions. It's the full power of their expressed Moxie that evokes those extraordinary gifts they've given to us and to future generations.

These passionate creators overcome and forge forward between failures, most of them much more quickly than those who allow themselves to be beaten up by the Inner Critic and other negative influences. This is the key difference between Being your grief, (the Inner Critic's policy), and Using your grief (the True Self's wizardry). You'll have obstacles to overcome and times of intense pain and confusion, but the pure innate powerful authentic being fortified by the Moxie within allows you to Master these circumstances rather than to be a Victim of them.

These extraordinary entertainers and creators are even able to reach inward and touch the center of their own truths and inspirations, and bring forth their pain, fears and triumphs as tools for creation. This heals. This teaches. This soothes. This empowers.

> *Spirit is what pushes people to accomplish the impossible. Rediscover your innate passion and life purpose.*

You don't often see masterful creators falter; you don't normally hear them whine. When is the last time you heard Steve Jobs whimper about a failed business deal? Or, have you ever heard Oprah Winfrey quibble on and on about anything? It's not that they don't have the audience, or that they don't want the attention. It's that they know, from past experience, that they can pull it out and pull it off, even though the process is often paved with doubt and fear. They use their Moxie to rise above.

They know it'll eventually end the way it was meant to, not always the way they planned, and that not everyone will love or even appreciate the end result. Their confidence and visionary fortitude come from their reliance on their inner truth for strength, endurance, truth, instinct and the hunger for bigger and better challenges. So empowered, people who create extraordinary results and lead extraordinary lives fully express their Moxie.

M = Mastery Minded
O = Opportunity Creator
X = X Factor: Your Authenticity
I = Intuitively Driven
E = Energetic Action

Actor Will Smith was one poor son-of-a-gun, as he would be the first to tell you. He worked his rear end off, exhausted, stressed and not really knowing what would come of his endless toiling. He worked by day and fine tuned his acting chops by night. He just knew he was a great actor, and that he had to keep acting, and that he had to keep facing rejection, humiliation, ignorance and exhaustion.

He just knew… just as you know that something lives inside of you. Something that is different from everyone else's something, and is worthwhile in every way. If you're always looking for or leaning on reasons not to do it, whatever it might be, you'll always find them. On the more productive and complimentary side—the Moxie point of view—if you're always aiming toward the step above the one you're on, you'll always find a way to mount it.

Even if you fall down two or 10 times before you get a good foothold, keeping that upward focus will make each trip, fall and misstep not only bearable, but exciting and useful. Winston Churchill, a Nobel Prize winning author, accomplished artist, powerful speaker and fearless defender of an invaded Britain during World War II, once said:

> *"Success is the ability to go from one failure to*
> *another with no lack of enthusiasm."*
> *- Winston Churchill*

Failure, or the way you perceive it, is not the end of anything. Failure is a positive affirmation that we need to go again from a different angle. Failure means a new beginning, one that's less uncertain with many possibilities for success. There's more than one way to do everything, and each failure brings you closer to the answer to your own riddle, puzzle, block or brilliant idea. If you embark on an adventure that ended without the desired prize, you can say definitively, "Well, at least now I know that way doesn't work. Let's try again, shall we?"

> *"I did not fail 1,000 times. I invented 1,000 ways not to make a light bulb."*
> *- Thomas Edison*

If you're worried about the amount of time it takes to "build an empire", you need not be discouraged. How old are you now? 33? 48? 67? It's been many years of you trying to figure out why you're so unsettled, confused, antsy, bitter, inconsolable, unfocused, restless, indecisive and downright frustrated. Going against nature has taken a far greater chunk of your time and stamina than following the flow of your nature ever will. When you give the world and the critics all the power, you never feel the full impact of gain or loss. There's someone or something to blame, so you don't learn much from your mistakes.

Similarly, you can never truly enjoy and feel uplifted by your accomplishments when you've relinquished power to "the gods, the powers that be" because they're chalked up to luck or fate. The only way to claim full bounty for everything you accomplish or fail is to Be True To Your Authentic Self! The downs aren't nearly so low, the ups are higher than you ever thought you could reach and the life you live is unique, free, exciting and best of all, It's Yours!

CHAPTER SEVEN

YOU SHOULD!

> *"To affect the quality of the day, that*
> *is the highest of arts."*
> *- Henry David Thoreau*

Of course, it doesn't always seem that simple where the demands and stresses of life come in to rain on your parade, but it actually is. All of life, every living and material thingy, is made up of energy. You've developed two very distinct energy receptors within your psyche. The first, your True Self, is that which you were born with, and it's never changed. It's replete with positive, light-seeking energy, and it pulls you toward everything playful, inspirational, magical, creative and new.

The True Self finds the positive energy in all things, even heartache and hardships, and uses it to help you dance when there's no music, sing when there are no lyrics, prance when the rest of the world is marching and recognize beauty even when it isn't pretty. The True Self is the calm, brave, gut feeling there to lead you to your inner calling, your unique self.

Your other energy receptor—I'm sure you'll recognize her by now—has been nurtured into you since before you could walk. She's learned that it's always safer to conform to mass standards, and that negative energy is the life source that keeps you from what it mistakenly believes will be painful or cause you to suffer.

She doesn't necessarily thrive on negative energy, because nothing really can. Because she's always seeking it as a means to an end, she allows it to encapsulate, intimidate and control you throughout your life's journey. As you now know, the Inner Critic projects, recognizes and envelops you in a misguided, protective coat of negative energy to hold you back. If she's successful, she'll render you unable to shine light in any area of your life. She's that part of you who believes that it's smarter and easier to be angry or stagnant than to take a chance on being hurt, and that it's better to be unhappily safe than to be happily standing on a potentially crumbly canyon wall.

> *"Those who can make you believe absurdities can make you commit atrocities." - Voltaire*

Your Inner Critic wants to keep you in the same place, doing the same things, with the same people, no matter how staggering or mundane, so you never have to float through the big bad world, venturing into unknown territory as a misunderstood, lonely, wacky, weird, crazy person. She'll tell you that you suck. She'll tell you that you can't make the living you want by pursuing your dreams. She'll tell you to get in line and shape yourself as other, smarter people tell you to.

You know those people, the ones who "should" on you constantly. (Yes, I meant shit. Both words produce the same anxiety and negativity.) They should all over you so much that you have to should on yourself when they're not around so you don't miss the constant, now comforting, drone of their drum beat. Before you know it, your entire life is just a great big steaming pile of should, and you feel buried and burdened by the weighty stench and mass of it all. Good goin'! Anything else you can do for yourself while you're down there wallowing in someone else's muck?

This is the first and often most hindering symptom of performance anxiety. There are people—perhaps you're one of them—who've never shown glimpses of their craft, their innovations, to anyone. There are those who don't even know they have a creative or entrepreneurial drive because they're so blinded by their Inner Critic that they couldn't see the value and the gift in their innate talent. Wait a minute. Not everyone can whip up a master plan or paint or think up newer and better ways of doing things for the betterment of all *effortlessly?*

The creative side of you, the True Self, is always at work in your gut, up and down your energy meridian and in your heart when you run across something that compels and inspires you. You may write a column or blog for your industry rag or website to make a living. Your work is stable, reasonable, practical, feasible ….and you're having a blast!

Your Inner Critic, however, can't recognize talent or flow when she reads such perfunctory material. Is this the best you can do? Is this all there is? You'll never rock your world with this drivel!

Your True Self sees your work as a stepping stone, a tool, an opportunity to learn, a good place to start. You've always loved writing, she says, and this is how you can develop your lexicon, improve your work, get feedback on your original material, expand upon your talent, get your foot in the door and have the Moxie to open and walk through even bigger doors! Be acknowledged as the go-to expert. Landing a placement on Oprah's Book Club list is only a matter of time!

Who wins? In the long run, will you obey your Inner Critic? Will you swallow the stories you really want to pursue so you can meet someone else's expectation by the end of the week? You could really use that extra 500 bucks. And just look at the reputable columnists and respected journalists and bloggers you're up against. You're not good enough yet, and you can't seem to break that glass ceiling that'll catapult you to the playing field of the rest of the best, so why bother stirring the pot? You don't need to pester your editor and secure a reputation as an unworthy front page chaser on their way out the door. Why risk your safe, secure position for a pipe dream?

> *"Without deviation from the norm, progress is not possible."* - *Frank Zappa*

Or, do you listen intently for the calm, playful, full of Moxie voice of your True Self over all the doubt, confusion, fear and competition—the voice that knows Richard Branson wasn't always known as *The One And Only Richard Branson*. The one reminding you 10 years ago you had no clue who Barack Obama or Ellen DeGeneres were. The tune you dance to is different, unpopular, unique, quirky, uncommon… that's what makes it so beautiful! Crank it up! Blow the speakers off the joint and let 'em know You're Here! You can do this, buck-a-roo, and you will! That's MO'XIE!

Your True Self delights in the excitement of the unknown, because she knows that as long as you're still breathing, there's still a chance of making magic. She's never boastful, condescending, comparative or nitpicky. She sees beauty in all of the world's energy, and she wants to share the positive reflections of her own energy with the world. She's grace, humility, strength, endurance and courage. And all you have to do is listen for and to her. Hers is the world of unlimited possibilities.

You were also conditioned to tolerate countless things that go against the nature of your authentic self, your inspired creative life. Tolerations are those circumstances and responsibilities you allowed to build up around you. As a naïve child, you often invited them in or just felt too tired or afraid to kick them out and clean these nuisances up for good. These tolerances come in many shapes, sizes and forms, but they all suck relentlessly at your precious energy. Since energy is what you need to sustain your body and mind, the more tolerances you put up with or invite, the less energy you have to focus on the authentic life you're supposed to be living.

Tolerations can be anything from meaningless, perfunctory jobs to unhealthy or abusive relationships, and everything in between. Every bit of thought, time, effort or energy you put into trying to work around, live with or coddle negative energy is a direct deduction from what your authentic self needs for fulfillment. Tolerations are distractions that take you away from who you are, what you want to do and where you want to go in order to gain the full potential of your authentic life.

> *"You have a masterpiece inside you, too, you know. One unlike any other that has ever been created, or ever will be. And remember… if you go to your grave without painting your masterpiece, it will never get painted. No one else can paint it. Only You." - Gordon MacKenzie*

Now, we all need a certain amount of money to survive. Basic physical needs are costly, and if you want to save or splurge a little, you'll need to have a—must I say it, dread the very thought, here it friggin' comes—J.O.B. to make sure you're Just Over Broke. Better get that job and be safe than risk everything on a wild business idea. So you say.

Some people marry it. If they're truly happy with their wedded partner that's great! Most soon realize that while money buys a lot of great stuff, it can't fill a hole deep within that's longing to be filled. No one else and no Prada dress can ever fill a hole in your soul.

You can end up spending more time job Hunting than you do job Finding. Sometimes you think you have to take whatever you can get, because people who can afford to pay you decently for your time and services are fewer and farther between than ever before, or so your Inner Critic has convinced you.

That said, you want to approach every new opportunity to make money from your True Self's perspective. Imagine what your life will be like when you're making a fortune doing what you love to do. Feels good doesn't it? Something about every job will tie into and inspire your creative, innovative True Self if you're looking at the job from her bright, curious and brilliant point of view. Most of all, she realizes that by staying focused and guided toward the next step up the majestic mountain, she can turn a stressful job into a rocket ship that will blast you over the rainbow of deep satisfaction.

If you don't like your job or career you have a choice. Either get a new job that inspires you or show up to the one you have with a renewed attitude and authentic contribution. If you don't make a choice the choice will be made for you in the form of a pink slip. Rather than allow yourself to be led into dark despair. take deliberate action to direct your bright future.

CHAPTER EIGHT

YOU'LL GET HURT!

> *"I dream for a living."* - Steven Spielberg

For some, dreaming is an escape, a hobby and a shout out to the universe for that which we're sure has escaped us. As children, our dreams incorporated the things that mom and dad thought were bad or dangerous, like crocodiles for best friends, French fries drenched in gooey cheese with a side of five layer ice cream sundae and driving race cars.

Most of us heard that the things we really wanted couldn't be afforded, or that what we longed for was immaterial, useless and unrealistic. Some of us were reminded that fine young ladies and gentlemen would never think of such things as proper. The remainder of us had nobody to tell us why; we just knew we had nothing but our dreams to fill the day. Eventually, we moved away from them, because without the tools, support and encouragement we needed, dreaming seemed to get us nowhere. We were collectively told to be part of the Real World, and so begun our cycle of unnatural conditioning.

What we did get was a fully paid, non-stop ticket to the land of confusion. Why did I have to play that confounded piano? Goodness sakes, I hated that thing. On my very best day I couldn't outplay an infant kangaroo, but I was dragged back to that bench day in and day out. It may have had something to do with the fact my mother was my piano teacher, or this was what prim, proper, clean, cordial, studious young ladies did... but I was cussing like a trucker inside. I couldn't even compose myself, let alone a piece of music, so why the torture? Now, give me a floor, level or not, and I'd dance your socks off! I was a Dancer. I Loved it. I Rocked at it.

So, how could she enjoy my slaughtering, pounding, groaning and lack of musical ability? And why is *To Kill A Mockingbird* acceptable reading material while *Lady Chatterly's Lover* isn't? And what makes Beethoven, an extremely controversial figure in his own day, more profound and revered than Led Zeppelin? Is spinach the only nutritious food known to man and will you die if you don't eat it? Is the piano the be all and end all of every good thing that ever entered our universe? Is it really politically and morally incorrect for a beautiful classic book to be honest about the times and titillating affairs of its subjects? Will my life be forever marred if I see the nude scene in the musical "Hair"? The answer to all of these questions, of course, is *Are You F#%king Kidding Me?*

> *"We are stardust, we are golden, and we've got to get ourselves back to the garden." - Joni Mitchell*

Parents see us as their responsibility and as an extension of the enslaved life they had wrapped around themselves. When locked up, slowed down, "have to" people have forgotten their dreams and have caged up the truth about themselves to sustain the impending life they've created, they forget how to look for and accept the real people around them. Where you see yourself as a happy, frolicking, good natured and fun-seeking little sponge, you're being introduced perhaps as I was as: "My messy haired, 11-year-old daughter. She nearly killed me coming out, and she hasn't stopped trying to torture me since."

As children, our fascination and love of life is either guided or encouraged by the adults around us, or it's unintentionally splattered and suffocated. Of course, as you look behind you throughout the journey, you may recognize a few instances when you did the splattering and suffocating yourself. (*It's okay, no judging here! Why waste good energy? You were a child doing the best you could.*) We're either accepted as beautiful and powerful, or we're misguidedly pounded into that which is acceptable and non-threatening.

Their own Inner Critic, who looked around at the safe, comfortable, predictable life they had earned and told them, "Now This Is Living", ruled my parents! It said, "Money, house, good-looking spouse, perfect kids... make sure they're perfect, or they'll mess up the whole package." It was their job to give me the "life they never had." I didn't know what perfect meant no matter how hard I tried, and it had become quite clear my parents didn't either, so who was I to be?

No time for lollygagging, artsy-fartsy hobbies, rebelliousness, hair dyed pink, toe-shoes dyed green, posters of longhaired freaks or any other form of personal, authentic expression. Those things make no money, they're precarious at best, and so few people will ever be good enough at these "recreational pastimes" to be successful. (Success = Money earned doing meaningful, important work to the Inner Critic.) Just suck the Moxie right outta me, why dontcha? Truth is, you and you alone are responsible for having the Moxie to express your True Self.

It doesn't matter what the financial stature is of your family. Those immersed in poverty depend on the Inner Critic to protect them and their families, as an imprisoning life of "must", "should", "have to" and "need to" is difficult to live. If life has been that tough for them, as hard as they've worked, then just imagine how hard it would be for you if you wasted good laboring and toiling time on whimsy and fantasy. Your parents think they're protecting you, they think they know best, because they come from a place of regret and fear.

Now that the cat is out of the bag, I'll mention that the Inner Critic is confused and intimidated by that which she can't see for herself. She likes to keep you safe, protected and exactly where you are, because she fears the unknown. She sees belongings, results, routine and obligations. If your parents didn't know anything about what you were doing, they couldn't control the outcome. This was something their Inner Critic wasn't willing to tolerate.

The Inner Critic in your parents berates them, reminding them constantly that they must control their children. The True Self on the other hand, is that clear, calm, positive, gutsy voice that we hear when something really turns us on. Full of Moxie, she can be mischievous, without a doubt, but she can also see the extraordinary within each person. She is instinct, inner power, happiness and drive.

Meanwhile, the clue that our parents were sending us, though they probably didn't even know it themselves, was just beneath the surface all the while… Dreams are Powerful! If dreams were merely puffs of smoke that float up to the heavens and dissipate with the clouds, why would they try so hard to talk us out of them? When you see a fire, you put it out, right? Well, a parent who sees your dreams as disappointments waiting to happen, as their parents saw their dreams as disappointments waiting to happen, wants to protect you from the unknown, the uncertainty, the disappointment that's attached to the uncharted territory.

Because they were talked out of or yanked away from their dreams, they don't know how to help you achieve yours. You say dream, they think naïve child… because that's the last time they allowed themselves to be free.

> *"All prosperity begins in the mind and is dependent only on the full use of our creative imagination." - Ruth Ross*

Because of an extreme misunderstanding and fear of all things innate and instinctive, "dream" to most conditioned adults has become merely a word that people use to romanticize a country, to sell things on TV or to explain the whimsy that happens during the sleeping hours. Dreams are rooted in the heart, separate from reality, and this is a frightening thought for those who are firmly ruled by the Inner Critic. Summarily dismissed as rubbish, nonsense and as utterly impossible.

This is fear, my friends. Simple, plain, staggering fear at play. Those ruled by the Inner Critic lead lives of quiet desperation or restless agitation. You might call it "empty hell" syndrome. It may appear that this person has everything in the world, yet there's sadness, or an underlying irritation, a reclusive quality or a feeling of unrest revolving around them. For those who are unfulfilled and lost, it's often the things that can be purchased that place worth on their lives. The more stuff, the more money and the more attention they get, the more value they think they'll hold for themselves. The more trinkets acquired, the more the "lie" the Inner Critic lack of self-worth is perpetuated.

The answer to low self-esteem must be in the getting of more! And the closets are filled with clothes never worn. Sometimes, in the undeserving-ness of it all, luxury cars are totaled; watches are lost and big estates empty of joy are sitting cold behind the gated community.

It's wonderful to have beautiful things, enjoy expensive pleasures and monetary comforts. I love my Manolo Blahnik's even though I can't walk in them! Total works of art—and they make my legs look great! What's not to love?

The problem arises when you look to the money and stuff to define who you are, to measure your success. Self-worth and self-esteem can only come from within.

> *"Money can buy you a fine dog, but only love can make him wag his tail."*
> *- Kinky Friedman*

The Inner Critic's common misconception about money is that money is the be-all and end-all to your problematic journeys. Those who don't have money tend to misjudge those who do, often criticizing and defaming their character just because of some numbers in a bank account. The Inner Critic deems "rich" people as a%#holes because they already have what she doesn't have and wants. The truth is, you may unconsciously fear having money because you don't want to be seen as a jerk, as a spoiled, lazy person—an a@#hole. You may also shy away from the pressures of money because of the false stigmas you place on those who do have it, no matter how they got it, what they do with it and most importantly, whether or not they are really a@#holes.

For example, you could decide that you want to be a movie star. You work hard, earn industry and public recognition and fulfill your promise. If you're showing up, engaged in your work, creating memorable characters and are authentically, genuinely happy with what you do, regardless of the money, then you've truly succeeded. If you've gone through all of these motions because they were expected of you, imposed on you or because you thought the money you would earn could thrill and fulfill you endlessly, then you've been misguided and smothered by your Inner Critic. Be mindful of the expectations you place on yourself and others. More importantly, be wary of those expectations imposed on you by the people in your life, including your Inner Critic.

One clue to determining whether or not you're living as your heart beckons or as your expectations dictate is how much energy you have. If you're chronically tired, you're working too hard at living up to everyone's expectations, including your own. You can get very, very good at that... but it's freakin' exhausting!

A person who's guided and strengthened by the True Self, on the flip side, is someone who draws you out effortlessly with optimism, inspiration and warmth. There's no intimidation, no feeling of unworthiness in their presence. The True Self is smart and kind enough to see the potential in all people, and is unafraid of complimenting and mentoring others. This person is strong, secure and powerful without confrontation or judgment. This is the person you are at your deepest core, and your True Self is charged and excited—completely energized—when you're united in alignment with your truth.

> *"Imagination is more important than knowledge. For while knowledge defines all that we currently know and understand, imagination points to all we might yet discover and create."*
> *- Albert Einstein*

When our elders and influencers fail to see the potential in their selves—and subsequently in us—we become unwitting extensions of them. We think we're meant to behave in a way exemplary of their hard fought stability. I was larger than life, they wanted me quiet. I wanted to go it on my own, they wanted me to relish in and be grateful for the opportunity to ride their coat tails. I wanted to be a heroine, I wanted to be good enough, and they didn't believe in me. They didn't believe in me because they didn't know who I was. They just knew who I should be and worked hard to help me get there.

In turn, I ended up forgetting who I was, too. I forgot just as my mother had forgotten and as her parents had forgotten before. Well-intentioned people pass their conditioning on, generation to generation—the fear of truth, failure, error and believing in dreams. They weren't allowed to live their dreams, so we won't be either. Too risky. Not Safe.

Money never reminded me, nor did a marriage and the divorce that followed, or traveling, or being involved at the forefront of one of the most important and universal tools known to man, the World Wide Web. What reminded me was an intrepid inner voice that saw me through, truth driven butterflies at the pit of my tummy, hints of excitement, calm through storms and those few people I'd met along the way who never changed because of expectations. Those whose lives expanded to reflect the authentic choices they made rejuvenated me.

As a child, I wanted to be a dancer. My perfect plan had me dancing until I was too old and wrinkly to dance anymore, somewhere around 25. (*I was sure my Grandmother was 25, and nobody wanted to see that in a tutu!*) I would then morph into my lifelong hero, Auntie Mame. Vivacious, confident, classy, larger than life, frightfully honest, hilarious, unpredictable in the most important ways, surrounded by interesting and colorful people, loved by many, often misunderstood yet loyally respected… she was everything I once felt about myself inside. There were those along the way who reminded me, without saying a word, that she still existed in my heart, and that she missed me terribly. Once I found the key and let her out for the world to see, the strength and bliss that was lacking through the better part of my life came flooding back in. Only... my version of her is all my own, dancing all around me, and it's even better than I had ever dreamed of. Such is the life of the authentically expressed self.

The years spent in my "should be" life were not in vain. I learned many valuable lessons along the way that continue to serve me to this day. Any moment spent lamenting what could have been is a moment wasted, a moment not spent deliberately planting a seed for what will be.

Which brings me to a gift that your True Self holds for you: FORGIVENESS. Holding grudges and perpetuating anger rather than releasing and learning from negative energy are just detrimental forms of resistance. Anger and resentment suck up so much precious energy, yet many people don't know what else to do with their emotions.

"If I stay mad," grumbles the Inner Critic, "then this will never happen again. I'll just build the wall up higher, close it in over my head, padlock it, deadbolt it, weld all the holes. Nobody Will Ever Get Us Again! Not Even You. You're not the Boss of Me!" And the wall grows higher, as fast as Pinocchio's nose. Okay. But, there are two pretty big problems with this... Can you breathe in there? And, uh, sorry to bring this up, but... How will you get out?

CHAPTER NINE

YOU'RE A VICTIM!

> *"Never be bullied into silence. Never allow yourself to be made a victim. Accept no one's definition of your life. Define Yourself." - Harvey Fierstein*

There's a simple formula your True Self wants to share with you… she's been trying to get you to bring forth the Moxie to get clear of that which imprisons you for a very long time. She knows you often hold the emotions of pain, resentment and anger. In the deep, dark place of all that doesn't feel good you're separated from her—and your light. Feelings that cut through and beat up on your heart are indicators that you're moving farther and farther away from that which you're here to experience.

Your feelings and emotions are natural signals that can be used to guide you or liberate you. As an energy source, they can be used to create or destroy. You can use your experience with pain and anger as tools in your toolbox to create moving and wonderful works of art, if that will communicate what you wish to express. Your True Self is always at your side to teach you how to move on from your despair. As tools, you might learn to let them go, put them away when you aren't using them to create with, so they don't become the tools that you use to build your personal life and experiences. There's a powerful lesson, even more transformational than the originating painful events. Her lesson, her secret formula, will lead you to the manifestation of all you desire, and ultimately, inner and outer peace:

Forgiveness = Unconditional Love = Freedom

Yes. It really is that simple. These few words are the key ingredients that go into a life lived freely, authentically and responsibly without pain or anguish. Now, I know that all painful circumstances don't seem simple when they're happening to you, and if you're a member of the human race, you'll certainly be bumped around a time or two by others or yourself.

Your Inner Critic has known this since she began protecting you all those many moons ago, and she reacts inappropriately when triggered by events reminiscent of the original onset of your chronic pain in order to avoid future and further painful disappointments. It's inconvenient to have your heart ripped out. It sucks royally to be misunderstood. It hurts something fierce when you suffer any kind of loss. You may also add on feelings of guilt and shame if you move on from tragic experiences such as the loss of a loved one.

Your Inner Critic thinks she can prevent, cover, protect, isolate, remove, hunker down, fight back and win out. And you wish she were right. In fact, you depend on her being right. You bought into her system of beliefs and thought patterns so you can continuously look at the events of your life in a way that will justify the very expensive purchase7. The problem is, your Inner Critic means well, but is rarely right.

How can you know when she's serving up misguided pain and anguish? It's easy. You don't feel good. You can't create. You can't fully express your vision on any form of canvas. You can't execute on the business side of your creative or entrepreneurial endeavors. You stand frozen, or you run away in hasty retreat, back to where you feel comfortable, even if that comfort zone is a blanket of pain.

"Unbeing dead isn't being alive." - e.e. cummings

Remember, the Inner Critic is all about protection—your protection, your safety. She's a culmination of all of the fears, perceptions, rules and procedures that have been presented to you, initially by your parents and other authority figures during times of pain, panic or difficulty. You've empowered her to make sure you navigate your life according to the misplaced knowledge.

Your Inner Critic views life and what's possible for you through the lens of mistaken protocol. Events are no longer mere events to be considered and acted upon rationally. Events, to the Inner Critic, become triggers, warning signals, which activate a rule designed to protect you. Scared easily for your safety, she takes heed of every situation that's not comfortable, and she magnifies it to the point where the original issue is no longer recognizable. She attaches made-up meanings to these events that create a fight or flight reaction within you. Any decision based in a fearful react will create an unwanted outcome.

> *"We all know, from what we experience with and within ourselves, that our conscious acts spring from our desires and fears." - Albert Einstein*

This is how you create your undesired experiences. Something happens, someone does or says something and you evoke a reaction. Your reaction is based on the automatic thoughts of the Inner Critic, and you respond accordingly. The trouble is, you react to the automatic thoughts—the attached meaning you give to the event—not the event itself. It's as if six people are taking the witness stand to give their account of the same traffic accident, testifying their truth from their vantage point and their frame of mind. Each version will be different, each experience a separate truth, though they were all present and saw the same event.

Stuff happens. What you have it mean about you and your life is the made up addendum brought to you by your faithful yet frightened Inner Critic.

Your Inner Critic uses your triggered reaction to hold you back as long as she possibly can. You hold on to the pain, anguish and anger by reliving it over and over in your head. Chronic discontent remains, and your Inner Critic wants you to hold onto that offensive feeling forever, misguidedly believing you'll never hurt that way again if she just keeps reminding you of what will certainly happen again.

You forget that what does happen is often very different and removed from what you thought would happen. In fact, what you think will happen rarely ever does. Most of what you fear never happens unless you create it yourself through your own self-sabotaging actions in obedience to the rightful Inner Critic. You are the ultimate, the divine creator of Your Life, good and bad.

> *"There are very few monsters who*
> *warrant the fear we have of them."*
> *- Andre Gide*

Hurt, pain, calamity, mistakes, self-inflicted hardship and destruction… any or all of these can happen to anyone, anytime, with no exceptions. Whether you're flying high and free or encapsulated in your imaginary little anti-life chamber, there's no way to escape being bumped and bruised by yourself and the outside world from time to time. What will really matter for you in the end is what you have these events and the misguided actions of others mean to you. You can let them lift you to a new level of appreciation and consciousness, or you can let them bottle you up, bog you down and close your heart.

How you experience the events of your life is your own doing, completely within your control and by your own choice.

Oppression or Opportunity: It's Your Call.

To keep you in the safe and familiar arms of your pain, your Inner Critic will deliver misplaced memories over and over again in order to give you someone else to blame for all that's not right in your life. People continue to blame their parents for the limited lives they live long after their parents are either gone or have no decision-making influence anymore. The judgmental voice of the parent, deceased or living, comes through the Inner Critic, who takes the place of the parent, dictating who you should be, what you should do and what you should have. If you're quick to anger, or shut down easily when faced with a challenge, you can just about bet that your Inner Critic has got your ass over a barrel inside.

The truth is, you've been hurt by people in the past, and may yet be again in the future. This is the reality of being a human amongst other humans, even when your intentions were pointed nowhere near targeting or harming someone else. You may differentiate your own troubles and woes as more devastating than those of others because something or someone precious was lost as the result of an "intentional" act by another person. You believe that you have more of a right to hold on to anger when you have to face the rest of your life without the person you lost or the innocence you long for. It's a way to continue to justify your ongoing robotic reaction. It keeps you from moving forward in any way, or allows you to hang on to your connection with someone you've lost.

Perpetuating your anger and pain in this way is you beating up on you. It's you who continues to create evidence (evidence = drama) in your life to justify your anger and pain. The big, fancy-schmancy term for this type of self-sabotage is "Baggage." This person or that person has too much baggage. You can't do this thing or that thing because you're too busy carrying your own heavy baggage everywhere you go. It weighs you down until you quit and give up trying out of sheer exhaustion.

> *"We are not held back by the love we didn't receive in the past, but by the love we are not extending in the present." - Marianne Williamson*

Nobody tied the 300-pound suitcase to your back. Nobody chained the dead weight to your ankles. Nobody is forcing you to wear that hefty emblem around your neck. Nobody is force-feeding you garbage on a stick day in and day out. And what's even more pressing is the fact that Nobody is suffering your perpetual anguish other than you.

If you blame your parents, anyone or anything else, for your discontent, you remain a victim, not taking responsibility for your life. And you'll continue to create more discontent. Until you realize that it's you who is perpetuating the anguish and you who have the power to create either anguish or pleasure, you'll continue to be the effect of the meanings you attach to the events of your life. You'll justify your unfulfilled life with "I can't because of (insert faulty person) or (insert blame at a thing)…" You'll find and assign excuses and reasons. You'll continue to live your life as a victim, a victim of your own Inner Critic.

You are the one who has empowered your Inner Critic, therefore, you can take her power back. The Inner Critic is a part of you, so you won't want to kill her any more than you would want to lob off your right arm. You just want to take her power over you away.

That's how you Moxie Up !

Disempower your Inner Critic! Empower your True Self! View your life, your experience, through that lens. Finally drop all that excess baggage you've been carrying around with you. Give it up already! How do you do that? Through forgiveness. Through having the Moxie to love yourself and others unconditionally. Even if you abhor the act, you can forgive the woefully misguided, in-the-dark person.

Yes, Forgiveness

Everyone is doing the best they can with the light they have to see. EVERYONE. That includes the hardened criminal on death row. Granted, some people are missing a few batteries in their flashlight. Nobody gets up out of bed in the morning wondering how he or she can screw up life that day. If someone does get up each day conjuring up how to screw up someone else's life, it's because they believe that the action will make their own life better in some way, keeping them safer. These destructive people live with an enormous, enraged, empowered Inner Critic at the helm, fearfully dictating their horribly ill-advised actions.

The people who've hurt you, wronged you and walked all over you, stole something precious from you, have their own lives to live, create and experience. They have to find their own way through the dark. As you do. You're just on different paths in the expansion of your self-awareness, growth and the actualization of your full potential.

You can shine more light upon your own personal journey with the understanding that everyone is connected through one common denominator: Doing the best they can—be it wisely or misguidedly, powerfully or as a victim. In that, we're all the same. Each and every one of us. Misguided acts can be forgiven with the knowingness that the individual who committed the act, including you, was just acting in the interests of the misguided Inner Critic. Forgiving the person is in no way condoning the act.

Forgiveness is a gift you give yourself to be set free from the act and its effect on you. There's no longer an external power to hold over you. The Inner Critic is stripped of the weapon she uses against your efforts to move on, and you're free to expand your possibilities.

"In a triangle, who is the betrayer, who is the unseen rival, and who is the humiliated love? Oneself, oneself, and no one but Oneself."
- Erica Jong

Holding onto your past is an insane way to live your life. Why? Well, let's take a look at the past.

I ask people, "Where is the past?" They most often respond with "It's behind me." Fair enough. So, I walk around behind them, peering, examining… "I don't see it back here? Where is it?" They more than likely laugh, redirecting my search to the brain portion of their anatomy. "It's in my head." "Oh, I get it now. So if I usher you into the operating room and ask the surgeon to remove the part of your brain with your past in it, he'd be able to find the past in your brain?" The scenario is often met with puzzlement and gives us a very strong basis for discussing the attachments and meanings to past events we carry around with that, "My past is who I am" mentality. Now they ponder the question, "If my past isn't behind me or in my head, just where the heck is it?"

The past only exists in the stories you tell yourself and others about it. More importantly, the stories you tell are based on your perception and interpretation, the lens through which you saw or heard the events. I ask parents if they've ever said or done anything that their children misunderstood or took out of context. The response to the question is always a resounding "YES!"

Now guess what they did as children? Guess what you did when you were a kid? Guess what you're still doing to this very day?

You're misinterpreting many of the events of your life.

Much of what you think is your past experience is based upon your misinterpretations. You were just a kid! You witnessed the events through the naïve eyes and understanding of a little child. You often didn't understand the context or the intention. You added whatever meaning you could come up with at your tender age so it would all make sense to you.

"Don't be stupid" becomes Rule #1: **I Am Stupid**.

"You can't make a living as a _____" becomes Rule #2: **If I Become A _____ I Will Not/ Cannot Make A Living.**

As you bump along, trying to understand how to fit into all of the smart adult code talk, your Inner Critic develops her "Rule Book" for you to live stringently by. By following her rules, you continuously look for or create new evidence to support the Rules: I Am Stupid and I Cannot Make A Living As A Writer/Dancer/Actress...

It's not your parents, or other early influencers, who hold you back from your desires. You, through your own Inner Critic, hold yourself back. With the best of intentions, you created your Inner Critic by mis-interpreting and generalizing your early experiences. Since you created her it is within your power to transform her.

Blaming others for your lot in life is living as a victim. Blame, Fault and Shame are Inner Critic virtues and have nothing to do with Living Responsibly. If you beat up on yourself in such a way or on anyone else, know exactly where the negative energy is coming from. Pay attention to how you think and what you say. If you're spewing negative swill upon yourself or others, you have allowed the Inner Critic to serve it up willfully.

Holding onto anger and resentment as a victim reinforces the be-havior that will continue to create a victimized life. You're powerless to deliberately create the experiences you want to have. You believe you have no control... and so, you don't.

> *Your circumstances are a mirror reflection of how you see yourself, your world and your opportunity.*

Even if your parents or caregivers did, indeed, do horrible things to you, they were doing the best they could. Perhaps they didn't even have a flashlight by which to see, so they were fumbling around in complete darkness, creating havoc every blind, misguided step along the way. If they knew how to turn on a light switch, or even where it was in all of the darkness, as means of brightening up their lives, they would've done it. They just don't know how or where. Parents have their own freaked out Inner Critics who continue to run their show, making sure the lights are kept out.

Forgiveness calls every single resistant behavior within you into play and forces you to reckon with yourself regarding all of the ways your Inner Critic is holding you back. Holding grudges and remaining hurt or angry is the best way to accomplish absolutely nothing. Moving from one form of resistance to another can become a depleting and exhausting way of life, a life unfulfilled, a story left untold. Resistance is the making of your stuck places, your creative blocks and your self-sabotaging behavior.

In that stuck, blocked or sabotaged place, you're manifesting your Inner Critic's deepest and most stringent survival tactics. It shows up in everything you do, even more so in the things you don't do.

Forgive

Acknowledge how you feel. Examine its hidden meaning. With compassion, let go of your pain and anger. Render it powerless to govern you. If you wish, you can tap into painful feelings as tools when you want to express such emotion through your artistic endeavors. Set them aside when they're not useful in creating the experiences you wish to enjoy.

Forgive. Let Go and Flow— with MOXIE.

Hold Unconditional Love.

For Others. For Yourself.

Your outer experience is merely a mirrored reflection of your inner experience.

If you feel like one of your cylinders is misfiring look within to discover where you are holding back your expression of love. It's true, when you live through love and compassion the world loves and has compassion for you.

Love is the generative power in the positive, healthy and abundant growth of the human spirit. Without love - beginning with self - the soul withers and dies. Doing and expressing what you love, rather than what you hate, is what will feed your soul.

If you need an example just take a look at today's media kabuki dance of fear and hatred. This frenzy only serves to stir up more dissatisfaction, anger and violence. Hate begets hate. Love begets love. If you want the world to be a peaceful and loving place you have to find it within yourself first. It really does begin with you.

Return to love.

> *"Be the change you seek." - Gandhi*

You can't get something if you don't already have it within you. You can't be respected if you don't have respect for yourself. You can't be acknowledged if you don't acknowledge yourself. You can't be loved if you don't love yourself. You can't achieve the future you desire if you don't see yourself living that dream.

In reality, you may have the love, respect and acknowledgement of others, but you won't feel or believe you do unless you hold those things true for yourself within.

Do you trust yourself? Do you love yourself? Are you happy with the company you keep when nobody else is around? By now, you see the way you perceive yourself. The way you care for and feel about You is the legacy and the light by which you reflect your Inner Being to yourself and to all people. It's the light by which you navigate your path, create your possibilities and express your vision.

Furthermore, the motivations you see in others are the reflections of the motivations you have within you. If you don't trust those you come in contact with without hard evidence of distrustful acts, it's because you don't trust yourself. If you believe other people or other things (the economy, the politicos, etc.) are out to get you, it's because you're out to get you, beating up on yourself time and time again.

What you experience in life is emanated from you and how you feel about yourself.

Know this: Where you say No to You is where you give your personal power over to anything other than yourself, including your Inner Critic.

> *"For of all sad words of tongue or pen,*
> *the saddest are these, 'It might have been!'"*
> *- John G. Whittier*

CHAPTER TEN

YOU'RE NOT LOVABLE!

> *"Promise me you'll always remember: You're braver than you believe, stronger than you seem, & smarter than you think." - Winnie The Pooh*

Ah, the Inner Critic. She's constantly measuring—measuring you, measuring others, measuring danger, measuring the probability of severe emotional storms, measuring the likelihood of unforeseen hazards, measuring the sheer mass of all failures rolled together, forming an eternal ball of doom and destruction. Sizing up the entire world, she's your lens to the world, her perception and her eyes. It's time to give that old bird some new glasses!

Her prescription is very outdated. Her measurement scale is broken. Her radar is askew. Her transmitter is scratchy and gets poor reception. Her captain's log of findings, your rule book, is laden with false information derived from corroded equipment and scribbled down illegibly into an old, tattered book with a missing cover and half of the pages worn out. It's time for new rules!

In her self-doubt and fear, your Inner Critic has made some extremely selfish and demeaning choices. She can't live them down because she judges you more harshly than she does anybody else, which causes her to behave even worse. She lives in fear and doesn't know what else to do! Your Inner Critic thinks that by finding fault with everything scary, and by beating up on others and on you, she makes herself feel better and safe. It never works, yet she'll continue to beat you into the ground, trying to justify and satisfy her egoistic needs. As with all things, there's another way to look at it. There's another side to your Inner Critic story.

> *"There are no facts, only interpretations."*
> *- Friedrich Nietzsche*

The wounded and frightened Inner Critic is a reflection of all of the meaning you attach to the pain, confusion and disappointment you've experienced, resist, fight and still struggle to block out today. Through the Inner Critic, you relive these moments over and over again in the stories you tell to yourself and whoever will listen to you.

The repeated mantras of "I'm not good, smart, funny, witty, talented, rich, young, brave, worthy, tall, short enough to have, be and do what I want. So, I have every right to Find Excuses And Reasons why I don't have what I desire, why I can't be and do what I dream of at my core. I've found justifications for why I can't pursue my life's calling—why I can't succeed at my inner calling. It's not my fault that I don't show up in my life each day as my authentic self. It's not my fault that I hold myself back each and every day!" That's a long-winded statement that packs a powerful punch. And it hurts.

> *"Every man dies. Not every man truly lives."*
> *- William Wallace*

Your Inner Critic hurts. She's lonely and cold and feels quite misunderstood. She dutifully protects you from what she fears to the best of her ability, yet rarely receives any credit at all. She's seen as monstrous, but is only trying to carve out a safe place for you in the huge, often seemingly frightening world. She's the misunderstood, gnarled up weighty part of you that you've created in order to keep you safe in your limited world. But, what kept you safe when you were little holds little relevance in the life you lead today.

The "You have to work hard for a living" rule works against you if you love what you do every day. You may spend hours and hours honing your skills and never think of it as working at all. You won't call it "work" because the more you focus upon your life's passion, the more energized you become. For you, your life's work is playtime. You enjoy it so much.

BUT you believe "work" is supposed to be depleting. It's supposed to exhaust and drain you. Therefore, you unknowingly work hard against yourself to make sure you can't, won't make a living out of just doing what you love. Your Inner Critic will step in to make sure that "making a living at what you play at" doesn't happen. You won't reach for the achievements you know will deliver your deepest desire. You'll blow, miss or ignore an opportunity that would have opened the door to your dreams. You'll sabotage the relationship with your editor, your boss, your agent or partner. And you'll beat yourself up and blame people and circumstances for all of it, to no avail. The whole pattern of behavior will begin again the very next day.

> *"We cannot solve our problems with the same thinking we used when we created them."*
> *- Albert Einstein*

There's an escape hatch to the maddening cycle of unwanted experiences. It's the doorway that leads you back to your beginning, the place where you can reframe all of your misguided perceptions and wonky thinking. That magical place is called Unconditional Love—Unconditional Love of Others, Unconditional Love of Self.

Weren't you listening when the Beatles sang, "All you need is love?" Perhaps you were too young to remember the wisdom of Jimi Hendrix when he proclaimed, "When the power of love overcomes the love of power, the world will know peace." Since I'm older than dirt I remember those lyrics and finally understand their full meaning and profound insight.

Unconditional love begins with accepting yourself and others completely, just as they you and they are in each moment, warts and all. It's embracing the unifying truth that everyone is doing the best they can and what they think is right. REMEMBER: *No one deliberately makes a bad decision to consciously create a bad outcome.* If deliberate actions are taken to hurt another person, it's in defense, and a misguided perceived protection of self that the action is taken.

I'm not condoning horrific actions. I'm not suggesting such feats are to be excused. While deploring the actions of that person, you can still hold love for the appalling and woefully misguided soul wandering around in the dark who Found Excuses And Reasons to make that loathsome choice. If you don't, your anger and hatred will eat you alive. Set yourself free of this tyranny.

Unconditional love of your self has to include love for the anxious and disagreeable Inner Critic. Yes, your Inner Critic is worthy of love. Why? Because no one ever gave her a flashlight. She's fumbling around in the dark doing the best she can. More importantly, love her because you created her in the first place. Loving and mindfully guiding your Inner Critic is loving yourself.

If you notice your Inner Critic having a temper tantrum visually sit her on your lap and ask her what is she not understanding. Let her express herself fully. Without judgment or ridicule, lovingly help her reach for a new perspective. Turn the tears of despair into renewed vigor for new possibilities.

Love with conditions attached can only cause more pain, more sorrow, anger, resentment and disappointment. Loving only parts of yourself means withholding your love for the other parts of yourself.

> *"It is what a man thinks of himself that really determines his fate."*
> *- Henry David Thoreau*

Where you withhold unconditional love in your life for yourself, for others, for your purpose, for the task at hand, is where you struggle in life. To set yourself free from these judgmental bonds, you must love unconditionally, forgive the misguided thinking and actions of yourself and everyone you know and everyone you meet. Unconditional Love means knowing and accepting that these things were done through misguided and monkey-minded Inner Critic thinking, and aren't in alignment with the greater good of anyone, including the perpetrator.

As you intentionally bring the thoughts of your Inner Critic out from the unconscious and into your conscious awareness, embrace her. Instead of beating up on her and her beating back up on you, stop the cycle with your unconditional love. You have the power to give that Inner Critic of yours a flashlight.

Use your imagination to give her a big hug, as you would a fearful or belligerent little child, to calm and soothe her. Thank her for all of the work she's done over the years to keep you safe. Let her feel safe in your arms. Let her know you love her unconditionally, and because you do, you'll take over the "book of rules" from now on.

In the beginning, you'll have to have this inner conversation more than a few times for reinforcement. With love, you'll set yourself free from the emotional and foolish thinking ties that hold you back from saying YES to your life, YES to your purpose, YES to You!

> *With self-confidence, the world bows to greet you and coincidence becomes your partner.*

Forgiveness and unconditional love intertwine; you can't achieve one without the other. Forgiveness of self, and therefore of others, is an ongoing process. Personal and professional growth is an expression of knowledge and self-awareness. Mistakes will be made. That's OK. Mistakes are merely steps along the way to success. If you beat yourself up for falling on your butt when you were learning to walk you would have given up on yourself. Just as you do now when you beat yourself up because you never learned how to walk, that is, to give yourself unconditional love. A mistake is just an opportunity to learn a better way of doing things, an opportunity to succeed.

> *"Our background and circumstances may have influenced who we are, but we are responsible for who we become." - Barbara Geraci*

Observe the True Self within you. This is the part of you that acts deliberately, never reacts. She has much to teach you about unconditional love. Have you ever heard her snap at or argue with your Inner Critic? Absolutely not. She has no reason to argue or fight with anyone. She has no urge to prove herself right. She simply shines her light brighter and brighter every day, eagerly learns each lesson and gets her magic done. She is pure, life affirming, explosively rich in color, powerfully positive energy.

It's impossible to feel any kind of negative energy when your True Self is in power. You've had those kinds of moments. Those are your "in the zone" moments, experiences when you're fully engaged in the experience at hand, when you have no sense of time, effortlessly expressing your authenticity, your full potential. You feel fabulous in those moments. There's no greater joy than to show up as who you were designed to be, doing what you were meant to do and having what you were destined to have.

Moxie Up! Empower your True Self and reconnect you to You. Show yourself what your entire life is meant be and who the real, complete you is. See through the lens of your True Self as you show the world her warm, inspiring light. Everything you need to fulfill all of your dreams, to successfully create your desired achievements and to find that place of inner peace and fulfillment that you long for, is already within you. Then think, speak and act in alignment with that True Self and what she longs for at her deepest core. Your True Self will Never, Ever lie to you and tell you "You Suck!"

CHAPTER ELEVEN

CONFIDENCE & COURAGE

You Rock!

Everything else you tell yourself is a lie. The voice of your misguided, frightened Inner Critic spews out fear and self-doubt to keep you safe, to hold you back from expressing your natural gifts and your purpose in life. Listen for and to that other voice within you, the voice of your intuition and inspiration—your True Self. Trust its wisdom, for its guidance is your birthright. With it, you have everything you need to be, do and have what you want in life. Use it, and Rock On!

You Most Certainly Can!

What will happen if you go for what you want instead of holding yourself back? You'll either succeed, or you'll find another way that doesn't work. Either way, you're further, smarter and more capable than you were before you tried. Keep Going! You Can, and You Will, succeed. Be willing to succeed. Be willing to fail. Both are steps in the direction of fulfilling what your heart is calling you to become.

You are YOU!

You are unique. There is no other being just like you. No one else can be you. You can't be anyone else. Your life experience is what you make it. All your experiences are a reflection of your innermost thoughts and beliefs. Shape your thoughts around what others believe to be true and you won't fit into your own shoes. Life will be uncomfortable for you. Walk centered in the truth of who you are at your deepest core. Skip merrily through life, even if you're skirting blocks and challenges. You learned the lesson from Dr. Seuss when he said, "Be who you are and say what you feel. Those who mind don't matter, and those who matter don't mind!"

You Are Good Enough!

Measuring one human against another makes about as much sense as pitting the moon against the sun. Each person is a unique and remarkable being, with his or her own gifts and personal powers. As the sun and moon are essential for life, each person has a unique contribution to make for the betterment of all and the continuation of life. Acknowledge who you are and follow your heart. The only one who can measure you is you (and your Inner critic lies!)

You Can Get Unstuck!

You don't have superglue on your feet that prevents you from moving forward. The only thing holding you back, keeping you stuck, is your scared sh#tless Inner Critic. You can free yourself from any imposed or self-created quicksand with the greatest of ease. Just change your thoughts. Reach for a new and better perspective, and on you go. Ask what your True Self wants to do and take one baby step in that direction. And then another. And another...

You Can't Fail Unless You Fail To Breathe!

Every moment of your life is a chance to start over. Each second that ticks by is a time when you have the choice between staying put or climbing, hiding or boldly exploring, whining or singing. Embrace your failures, for they come with wonderful gifts in the lessons you learn from them. When examined, each failure contains the data for what didn't work and why. With this new knowledge, you can create better strategies and approaches, or even pave completely new roads to get to your goal. Without the failure, you wouldn't have the key piece of information! So if you fail, fall squarely on your butt and say, "Woo-Hoo! I get to learn something! I'm on my way to success!"

No More Should-ing Allowed!

Any time you make choices based on what your Inner Critic tells you to do, based on what she's heard others say you "should" or "shouldn't" do, you Should all over yourself and end up in a stinky mess. When you tell others what they Should do, you should all over them with your expectation that they be in perfect alignment with your thoughts and beliefs. The expectation is as unrealistic as the expectation that you be in perfect alignment with the thoughts and beliefs others hold. Expectations between people are merely Inner Critic battles for power. Each fights to reign supreme over the other lest its own misguided beliefs be challenged. Instead, base your choices in life on the voice of your intuitive True Self. Act from inspiration rather than from fear. Inspire those around you to do the same.

Your Emotions Indicate Your Life Direction!

Are you moving closer to or further from expressing your unique and full potential? It's very easy to determine where you are and what direction you're headed toward in your life experience. Just check in with how you feel. If you feel good, you're headed in the direction of your dreams. If you feel bad, afraid or have self-doubt, you're facing and heading the wrong way! Events in and of themselves don't cause pain, stress or anxiety. What you believe those events mean about you is creating your pain. Be mindful of the meanings you attach to the events of your life. Challenge them for truth versus Inner Critic misguided perception. Reach for a better thought.

You Are A Powerful Being!

You were born a victim of no one and no thing. While you depended on others to feed and take care of you as a young child, you always had your own power, unless you gave it up to someone or something else. The only one who can victimize you is You! You are that powerful! With this power, you create every experience you have. You can create your life experience deliberately with intent, or you can let go of your power and let life happen to you.

Unfortunate events do happen. Joyous experiences happen as well—each one is your own creation. There is an important distinction between and event and an experience. An event is an occurence. Illness, war, even horrific affronts to your safety and security are merely events. The experience is the emotional reaction to the event. While you did not create the event, how you experience those events *is* your creation.

A tragedy happens. A child is killed by car driven by a drunk driver. One mother will crawl under the proverbial bed in misery and hatred the rest of her life. Another will do as Candace Lynne Lightner did and create Mothers Against Drunk Driving. The impact of her message led to a dramatic change in public attitudes toward drunken driving, which was once the only acceptable form of homicide to socially unacceptable and severely punished as a crime. Her motivation was not hate driven; it was to make the world a better place.

If you have an *experience* you don't like, ask yourself, "What within me created the way I'm reacting to what happened?" Distinguish between real grief over the tragedy, as in Candace's case, and how it shaped your life moving forward. In your examination, leave judgment at the door. Judgment has no place in self-examination. Judgment is the work of your lying Inner Critic!

As you self-examine, you'll identify the thoughts that led to the choice you took action upon, which created the unwanted outcome. Did you weaken or did you find a way to tap into your inner strength? If you ran away what could you have done instead to create a better result? Now you're armed with the information to revise or reframe the thoughts and beliefs that created the experience you didn't like.

If you have a good experience, look within to discover the thought patterns that created the good experience. Now you have the recipe to create a similar good experience any time you choose! You're a powerful Moxie Master after all! You can mix up any potion to create any experience you choose!

Yes, I know, I know. Your Inner Critic is screaming, "Well, how am I responsible for 9/11 or a sick child?!?!" Tragic events on a grand scale indeed! Again, how you experience these events is of your own doing. One person will use the event completely withdraw. Another person will use the event as an opportunity to rise above.

A global catastrophe or untimely death of a child is a profoundly sad event. We don't know what that child's purpose in life was. If such an occurrence happens in your life, look for the gifts, the life affirming lessons embedded within that experience. Perhaps that child's purpose was to teach you and others to appreciate life and health. Honor the child and her gifts by living your life through the lessons you learned in that child's presence. Honor your purpose, your power to create all that is life affirming.

You Got Da Power!

You ARE Love!

Simply put, you are the manifestation of love. You're here to love and be loved. Where you hold back your love of self and others is where you struggle. Unconditional love is love without condition. You, and everyone else, are doing the best they can with the light they have to see. Some shine more light than others. Some live in the sunshine of life, others have wandered into the dark and can't find any light. All are doing their best.

With love and compassion for yourself and those you meet, your world becomes a safe place. Lies are brought into the light and the truth is revealed. Lies give way to truth. You are Love. You are Powerful. You are the light of pure love energy.

You are here to achieve authentic greatness with unrelenting drive and passion. This is your purpose. In doing so, hold unconditional love within you and it's expressed through your Higher, True Self, your Inner Being, the Divine or whatever you choose to call your true energy. Tap into this powerful energy. Follow its guidance through inspiration and intuition to bring forth into the world your masterpiece—the actualization of your full potential.

See yourself as I see you. You are truly special. A superstar!

"Who in the world do you think you are? A Superstar? Well how right you are!" - John Lennon

I would like to suggest that you take a moment to imagine how you would feel if you showed up in life as whom you really are going after what you really want. Boldly live life on your own terms, out from underneath the expectations of others, including your Inner Critic. That's Moxie! To find out how you can start to Moxie Up! to have the confident courage to achieve authentic greatness with unrelenting drive and passion, go to http://www.MoxieTheapy.com today!

SPECIAL BONUS

MOXIE SELF-ESTEEM WORKBOOK

Contents

Introduction

When was the last time you looked in the mirror and truly saw your Self? Did you notice joy dancing in your eyes? Or the evolution of the person you've become? Or were you afraid to look too closely, fearing something you might not like?

If you had a bad reaction to your reflection, you were looking straight into the eyes of your Inner Critic. And she's a gnarly thing, indeed!

You know you're looking at the *real* you, when your image purrs back, "Damn! You are too beautiful for words, my dear!" You *embrace* the gorgeous ways life has etched itself upon your precious face.

That is your True Self reflecting back at you—a confident person full of Moxie who lives in your heart, embraces life and all the facets of your being.

You were born with inherent goodness. That's right, **you are fundamentally good**—period! You came into this world with pure truth in your soul. It's the source of your power.

*Somewhere along the line, as you grew from a child to a teenager to an adult, you gave up some of this inborn power. Your truth was slowly whittled away. Unknowingly, you gave away bits and pieces of your natural expression in exchange for people pleasing and perceptions of survival. You lowered yourself in your own estimation and in turn, your self-esteem took a hit. **You lost your Moxie!***

The Real Definition of Self-Esteem

Self-esteem is much more than pride in oneself or self-respect. Self-esteem is about confidence in your ability to think and cope with the basic challenges of life. It's the belief that you're worthy, you're entitled to declare and achieve what your heart is calling you to become.

That's Moxie!

People with high self-esteem:

- Know that they're **worthy of happiness**
- **Trust** their own intuition
- **See and master opportunity**
- **Respect others** and are **respected in return**
- **Are confident, focused and present**
- **Boldly express** their selves with grace
- Have the **confident courage** to achieve **authentic greatness** with unrelenting drive and passion.

People with low self-esteem:

- Go through life miscast in the story of their life
- **Accept abuse**, exploitation and degradation from others, in subtle or overt ways
- Are motivated primarily by **fear**
- Are **victims** of self-sabotage and their circumstance
- Rely on their Inner Critic to keep them away from what they really want in life

Having self-esteem and self-confidence in oneself is essential for being happy and fulfilled in relationships. Your self-esteem, whether it's high or low, will generate self-fulfilling prophecies. *Have the **Moxie** to create what your heart is calling you to become!*

Is there such thing as having too much self-esteem?

NO!

It's impossible to have too much self-esteem just as you can't have too much health. Having high self-esteem is not the same thing as being arrogant, a braggart or conceited. Such characteristics reflect an *unhealthy self-esteem* rather than a healthy one. Arrogance, bragging and conceit are the language of the **Inner Critic**.

People who have high self-esteem don't feel superior to others. Their value is not measured against others at all. They're in touch with their **True Self** and know, with certainty, and who they really are.

Those who have high self-esteem often threaten people with low self-esteem. The Inner Critic is threatened and rendered powerless when in the presence of the True Self. When people with low self-esteem declare a person has "too much self-esteem," they're really making a statement about their own *lack of self-esteem*.

Low self-esteem can have devastating consequences:
- It creates stress, anxiety and depression
- It harms professional and personal relationships
- It can seriously impair job and academic performance
- It can lead to increased vulnerability to drug and alcohol abuse

Worst of all, these negative consequences reinforce the feelings of low self-worth and take you into a downward spiral of lower self-esteem and increasingly non-productive or even actively self-destructive behavior.

Steps Toward Creating Moxie Self-Esteem

So, how can you improve your self-esteem? How can you freely express your True Self instead of letting your Inner Critic do all the talking?

RELAX!

Where you are now is the only place you *can be!*

When you hear words of discouragement entering your thoughts or coming out of your mouth, ask yourself, "Whose voice is that?"

Are you hearing the voice of a mother, father or other relative? Perhaps it's the voice of a disapproving teacher who didn't seem to believe in you. Usually, it's many voices combined, all emanating from your **Inner Critic**. And right now, she's holding your power and guiding your life choices.

If you've bought into these words, you could be suffering from a case of spiritual stolen identity. Actually, your identity wasn't stolen—you freely took your power from your **True Self** and gave it to your **Inner Critic**, by allowing people's opinions of you to slowly shape your personality. You gave up your Moxie!

One of the things I've noticed over the years is that people tend to get stuck in the gooey residue that others have placed before them. They've bought into a picture of themselves that others have painted.

They contort and misshape their **True Self**, based on other people's needs and expectations. It's like walking into a mirror maze at a funhouse and not being able to find your way out. Everywhere you look is a twisted version of you that you don't truly recognize. Some people understand that the way to get out of this maze is to stay centered and focused. Others get stuck there, hoping that someone or something will rescue them.

Self-worth comes from learning to *embrace your self—wholly and with unconditional love.* That's MOXIE! If you want others to love and respect you, then you first must love and respect yourself. I don't mean you need to go around hugging yourself like people did in the 70s (although this can be a good idea!) But I do mean embracing the truth of who you are and bring it fully into the world, without fear or shame.

Uncovering the Real You

Finding out who you really are and acting from that place can be a little scary and awkward at first, but it will also bring a lot of relief. The charade is over! You no longer have to alter your **True Self** for the sake of others. The cat is out of the bag!

With more practice, you'll begin to rely more on your **True Self** and open up to more of life's possibilities. You rediscover your **True Self** and embrace it…and then you laugh. You laugh like you've never laughed before because you realize how funny life really is and how you've ignored so much.

Look into your heart in times of uncertainty that's where you will find the treasures of your soul!

The Moxie Self-Esteem Workbook Exercises

Lesson 1: Get to Know your Inner Critic

Your **Inner Critic** has been chattering endlessly in your head, beating you down and telling you over and over again that you're not_____ enough (fill in the blank.)

Carry around a journal or a note pad and jot down each statement your **Inner Critic** says to you during the course of a day. At the end of the day, review this list and REBUT every statement.

Ω If the **Inner Critic's** statement was harsh ("It's only a matter of time before they realize I'm a complete idiot."), rebut it with a reassuring statement. ("They must have confidence in my abilities or they wouldn't have asked me to do the job.")

Ω If the statement was unrealistic ("You never do anything right!") be specific. ("I do a lot of things right. I just slipped up on this one occasion and learned a valuable lesson from it.)

Ω If the statement was a leap in logic ("He doesn't look happy. He must not like me.") challenge the logic. ("I don't know why he doesn't look happy. It could have nothing to do with me. Maybe I'll ask.")

Ω If the statement was catastrophic ("He didn't hire me. I'll never get hired! I'll end up living in a box by the side of the road!) be objective. ("Well, I didn't get that job. That doesn't mean I'll never get a job. There's just a better job for me out there somewhere. All I have to do is find it!)

Lesson 2: Spread a Little Golden Rule

Treat yourself as you would like others to treat you. Why consider yourself any less important than anyone else? Take care of your physical needs—a healthy diet, regular exercise, good hygiene, etc. Practice relaxation. Experience fun.

Ω   What is one destructive habit you could replace with a good one? (Choose a piece of fruit instead of a doughnut for breakfast.) Do it!

Ω   Treat yourself to something special. You *are* special after all, aren't you! Would you like to get a massage? Or start that garden you've always wanted? Take an afternoon and do something just for you—even if it's just to relax and take a nap! How do you feel when you do something for yourself?

Lesson 3: Crown your Own Achievements

Notice all the things you're able to accomplish in a week. Heck, you did several things right just to make it through an average day! Reward yourself for your accomplishments. The reward can be something as simple as patting yourself on the back or taking yourself out on a "self-date" to a movie you've wanted to see. Spend your time noticing what you *do* rather than what you *don't do*. Notice any changes you experience with this new focus.

Make a list of all of your strengths and achievements. Write down everything you like about yourself. When you've completed this list, ask your friends, loved ones and associates what they like about you. Notice how you feel when you create this list. Keep this list close at hand to review often as a reminder of who you *really* are.

Lesson 4: Let Your Inner Critic Speak

Write down a list that begins:
"The things I don't like about myself are...."
List everything you can think of. Don't censor. If the thought comes into your mind, write it down. When you're finished, look at your list and ask yourself:

- Where did these beliefs come from?
- Is there positive or negative energy around that belief?
- Who said these things to me or about me?
- Do I want to believe these self-criticisms anymore? Or am I willing to let them go for the sake of my own well-being?

Now cross all the statements off your list that that someone else has created — those that are merely echoes of what others have said about you. Then cross out all statements that are negative. That's only one perspective. Replace them with a newer and more positive viewpoint. Next cross out all the statements you use against yourself *based on the way other people's behavior makes you feel.* You may also decide to give up the others as well. Because guess what? Who needs them?!

Now imagine the paper represents an old part of your self-image that you no longer want. Destroy this page, and as you do, concentrate on letting go of those negative messages.

Remember:

Forgive yourself when you don't accomplish everything you intended, even when working on these exercises. If the Inner Critic gives you a hard time, consider it a learning experience rather than a lesson in defeat. You're doing the best you can. You're always learning and improving. This, too, is an opportunity to learn and grow.

Lesson 5: Show Up Differently

How you "show up" in the world is based on how you feel and the stories you repeatedly tell yourself. Dare to muster up your Moxie and reach for a thought that makes you feel better when you're not feeling so good about yourself. If you don't like how people are treating you, change how you "show up" by creating a thought or a story that makes you feel good instead!

Think of the person you admired as a child. How would that person handle your circumstance? Remember, who and what inspired you, as a child, is a reflection of who you are. Act as if you were that person. What would he or she think and do? At least take a step in that direction. It will give you the courage to take the next step and the one after that. Before you know it you're feeling good about who you are. People are treating you with the same healthy respect you are giving to yourself.

Lesson 6: Change the Story, Change your Life

Your self-image is based on the story you've told about yourself over and over again. Life is an ongoing journey. It's unlimited in the number of new experiences and new stories you can create. It's time to rewrite your story.

Ω   Take a few minutes now and write down two personal stories that have impacted your life and helped shape who you are.

Ω   What kind of stories are they? Are they dramas? Love stories? Comedies? Mysteries? Thrillers? Tragedies? What meanings have you attached to these stories? How have they shaped your view of people, relationships, vocations and your future?

Ω Do these stories represent what really happened? Write the stories from the point of view of the other people involved. What else could the story mean? Does this change your perspective at all? If so, how?

Ω Now write the story based on the way you'd like your life to unfold. What new types of people would you like to include in your "cast of characters"? Which old characters would you like to see in different roles? What would be the greatest outcome of this new story? Be bold. Express your **Moxie**!

Ω How does this new story make you feel? What's now possible with this new story that wasn't possible before?

Ω Write down any insights you had while doing these exercises. How has your image of yourself and your opportunities in life changed?

Claim Your Truth. Own Your Power. Command Your Stage

MOXIE UP Your Self-Esteem!

Now that you know you're worthy and deserve the life you've longed for deep down inside, take decisive action to **LIVE AUTHENTICALLY OUT LOUD**. I invite you to schedule your Personal Moxie Up! Consultation today! Imagine how you'll feel when you confidently take advantage of a personally designed program to achieve your authentic greatness.

Go to www.MoxieTherapy.com or email Valery@MoxieTherapy.com.

If the beat of the Inner Critic kabuki dance is creating havoc with your life today it's time to change the channel.

Claim Your Truth • Own Your Power • Command Your Stage

www.MoxieTherapy.com

In order to achieve extraordinary success—a life, career, business or relationship that rocks your world—you have to have the confident courage to go after what you really want: to achieve authentic greatness with unrelenting drive and passion. To do that you have to muster up your Moxie!

One of the things you're really going to love about the Moxie Up! Program is the feeling of power and control you have over your life experience.

Moxie Therapy is not for everyone. As your personal Moxie Master and stuck places troubleshooter, I don't give boilerplate advice or offer canned coaching programs. I'm fully invested in helping you get what you want. To do this, I may say things or challenge you in ways that make you uncomfortable. I'll shake it up as I teach you how to look at your creative expression and your life from different viewpoints and expanded perspectives.

You'll be treated with love, respect and without judgments. The process is stimulating and we'll have some fun! You can do it—get well on your way within 90 days—if you really want to make an empowering difference in your life.

Get started today! If not now, when? Your extraordinary life is waiting.

ABOUT THE AUTHOR

Valery Satterwhite is an Author, Speaker and Expert Moxie Master. She has extensive training in emotional intelligence and behavioral transformation techniques. She's Master level certified in Neuro-Linguistic Programming (NLP) and Emotional Freedom Technique (EFT). She's also a Certified CORE Multidimensional Awareness Profile Facilitator. In her role as Moxie Master and Creator of Moxie Up! at www.MoxieTherapy.com, Valery offers discerning individuals who demand personal attention her meticulously designed Moxie Up! process. Her custom consultations are designed to help you quickly reconnect with your authentic self, get out of your own way and infuse vitality and purpose into your life. You'll become the extraordinary master of opportunity rather than an empty victim of circumstance.

A 20-year digital media veteran, Valery was one of the pioneers of the Internet industry, working closely with the entertainment industry as a Senior Level Executive and President of various interactive media entertainment emerging technology companies. While successful in her corporate career, Valery's heart and spirit always longed to break free. She longed to live boldly, authentically and courageously.

Stuck in this tired, albeit successful, career Valery would often laugh and say she wished she could be who she longed to be when she "grew up". Valery's childhood idol was the semi-fictional character "Auntie Mame", a larger than life woman who stood center stage, confident of her own truth, who loved and lived a rich and delicious life, while encouraging others to do the same. Valery learned from Mame that if she wanted to take charge of her own destiny and command her stage, she would have to change her life to align with who she truly was at her deepest core rather than who the world told her she "should" be. In this moment of awareness, the heart of www.MoxieTherapy.com was born.

Valery will teach you how to Moxie Up! Her definition of Moxie is: The confident courage to achieve authentic greatness with unrelenting drive and passion. Claim your truth, own your power and command your stage—on your own terms. Moxie Up! Bring out the bigger, more vibrant and expressive person within you that you know is there. Your very soul is calling. This is your purpose.

Will you answer this call?

NOTES

Notes

Notes

NOTES

Notes

YOU SUCK!

Notes

NOTES

Notes

YOU SUCK!

Notes

NOTES

Notes

www.ingramcontent.com/pod-product-compliance
Lightning Source LLC
Chambersburg PA
CBHW060938040426
42445CB00011B/913